MERS "OLYMPIC" AND "TITANIC".

PLATE III.

SHELTER DECK C
SALOON DECK D
UPPER DECK E
MIDDLE DECK F
LOWER DECK G

BOAT DECK

PROMENADE — OFFICERS PROMEN—
OF OVER
1ST CLASS
ELEC WINCH
CHIEF OFF.
BOILER CASING
BOILER CASING
HOUSE
GYMNASIUM
ENTRANCE
ELEC WINCH

PROMENADE DECK A

FIRST CLASS
READING AND WRITING RM
FIRST CLASS
3
3
BOILER CASING
BOILER CASING
CORRIDOR
ENTRANCE
3
3
ENADE

TITANIC

THE COMPLETE BOOK OF THE MUSICAL

Story and book by

PETER STONE

Music and lyrics by

MAURY YESTON

Photographs by

JOAN MARCUS

AN APPLAUSE ORIGINAL

TITANIC:
  THE COMPLETE BOOK OF THE MUSICAL

Copyright © 1997, 1999 by Peter Stone and Maury Yeston

  Story and Book by Peter Stone
  Music and Lyrics by Maury Yeston
  All Production Photographs Copyright © by Joan Marcus
  Scenic and Costume Designs Copyright © Stewart Laing
  Historical Photos courtesy of The Illustrated London News Picture Library
  Artwork Production Identity by Doug Johnson ©1997
  All images and artwork of the production supplied through the courtesy of Dodger Endemol Theatricals

The Author and Publisher gratefully acknowledge the full cooperation of Actors' Equity Association, Kimberly Russell for her caring research and Jane Gelfman without whose enterprise this book would never have happened.

Author's Note: All characters and events in *Titanic* are based on fact. Dramatic License has been taken only when the specific facts were unknown.

  ISBN 1-55783-355-9 (cloth)
  ISBN 1-55783-376-1 (paper)

Designed by Graffolio
Printed by Tucker Printers
Bound by The Riverside Group

First Applause Printing: 1999

Library of Congress Cataloging-In-Publication Data

  Library of Congress Catalog Card Number: 98-89566

British Library Catalogue in Publication Data
  A catalogue record for this book is available from the British Library

APPLAUSE BOOKS

211 West 71st Street
New York, NY 10023
Phone (212) 496-7511
Fax: (212) 721-2856

10   9   8   7   6   5   4   3   2   1

CONTENTS

CAST
Officers & Crew of R.M.S. Titanic

Capt. E.J. Smith...John Cunningham
1st Officer William Murdoch...David Costabile
2nd Officer Charles Lightoller...John Bolton
3rd Officer Herbert J. Pitman..Matthew Bennett
Frederick Barrett, Stoker..Brian d'Arcy James
Harold Bride, Radioman..Martin Moran
Henry Etches, 1st Class Steward...Allan Corduner
Frederick Fleet, Lookout..David Elder
Quartermaster Robert Hichens/Bricoux...Adam Alexi-Malle
4th Officer Joseph Boxhall/Taylor...Andy Taylor
Chief Engineer Joseph Bell/Wallace Hartley..Ted Sperling
Stewardess Robinson..Michele Ragusa
Stewardess Hutchinson..Stephanie Park
Bellboy..Mara Stephens

Passengers aboard R.M.S. Titanic

J. Bruce Ismay..David Garrison
Thomas Andrews..Michael Cerveris
Isidor Straus..Larry Keith
Ida Strauss..Alma Cuervo
J.J. Astor..William Youmans
Madeline Astor...Lisa Datz
Benjamin Guggenheim...Joseph Kolinski
Mme. Aubert..Kimberly Hester
John B. Thayer...Michael Mulheren
Marion Thayer..Robin Irwin
George Widener..Henry Stram
Eleanor Widener..Jody Gelb
Charlotte Cardoza..Becky Ann Baker
J.H. Rogers..Andy Taylor
The Major..Matthew Bennett
Edith Corse Evans..Mindy Cooper
Charles Clarke...Don Stephenson
Caroline Neville..Judith Blazer
Edgar Beane...Bill Buell
Alice Beane...Victoria Clark
Kate McGowen..Jennifer Piech
Kate Murphey..Theresa McCarthy
Kate Mullins...Erin Hill
Jim Farrell...Clarke Thorell
Frank Carlson...Henry Stram
Other Passengers..Charles McAteer

UNDERSTUDIES

Drew McVety (Barrett/Bride/ Hichens/Boxhall/Rogers/ Farrell)
Andy Taylor (Barrett/ Lightoller/Clarke)
John Bolton (Bride/Murdoch)
Jonathan Brody (Fleet/Bell/Hartley/ Lightoller/Hichens/Farrell/ Thayer/Guggenheim)
Peter Kapetan (Bell/Hartley/Murdoch/ Ismay/Beane/Astor/

Guggenheim/Thayer/ Guggenheim)
John Jellison (Boxhall/Rogers/Pitman/ Major/Capt. Smith/Beane/ Astor/Straus/Thayer/ Guggenheim)
Joseph Kolinski (Smith/ Andrews),
Matthew Bennett (Ismay/ Andrews)
David Costabile (Ismay/Etches)
Henry Stram (Etches)
Lisa Datz (Kate McGowen/Caroline Clarke)

Theresa McCarthy (Kate McGowen/Caroline Clarke)
Melissa Bell (Kate Mullins/Kate Murphey/ Aubert/Mrs. Astor)
Kay Walbye (Mrs. Widener/ Mrs. Thayer/Mrs. Beane/ Mrs. Straus/Mrs. Cardoza)
Jody Gelb (Mrs. Beane/ Mrs. Straus)

SWINGS
Melissa Bell, Kay Walbye, Jonathan Brody, John Jellison, Drew McVety

Dodger Endemol Theatricals
Richard S. Pechter
The John F. Kennedy Center for the Performing Arts

present

TITANIC

A New Musical

Story and Book by
PETER STONE

Music and Lyrics by
MAURY YESTON

Scenic and Costume Design
STEWART LAING

Lighting Design
PAUL GALLO

Sound Design
STEVE CANYON KENNEDY

Orchestrations
JONATHAN TUNICK

Music Supervision and Direction
KEVIN STITES

Music Coordinator
JOHN MILLER

Casting
JOHN HUGHES & BARRY MOSS, CSA

Technical Supervisor
AURORA PRODUCTIONS

Action Coordinator
RICK SORDELET

Production Stage Manager
SUSAN GREEN

Executive Producer
DODGER MANAGEMENT GROUP

Press Representative
BONEAU/BRYAN-BROWN

Marketing Consultant
MARGERY SINGER

Associate General Manager
ROBERT C. STRICKSTEIN

Choreographed by
LYNNE TAYLOR-CORBETT

Directed by
RICHARD JONES

Previewed from Saturday, March 29; Opened in the Lunt-Fontanne Theatre on
Wednesday, April 23, 1997.

Winner of 1997 "Tony" Awards for Best Musical, Score, Book of a Musical,
Orchestration and Scenic Design.

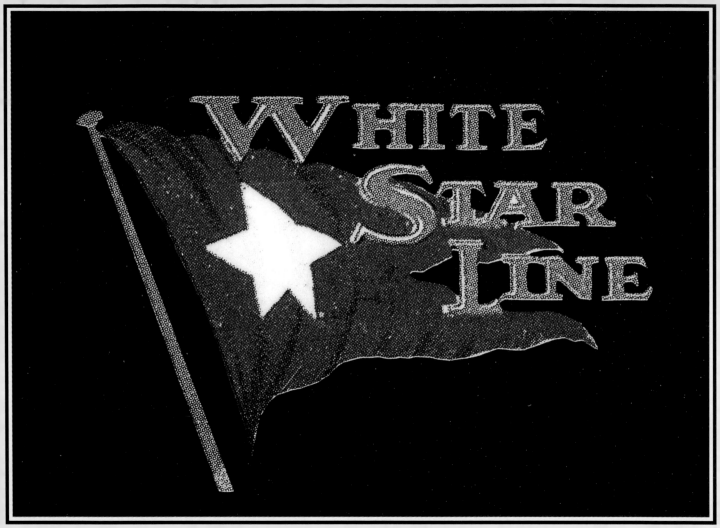

How Did They Build *Titanic?*
Peter Stone

R.M.S. TITANIC, the crown jewel of Britain's White Star Line, was, when she was built, the biggest, strongest, finest and grandest ocean liner ever conceived by man. She was quite literally THE LARGEST MOVING OBJECT IN THE WORLD. Eighty-five years after the purportedly unsinkable ship hit an iceberg on her maiden voyage and went to the bottom of the North Atlantic, her story is still being told, and still widely embraced by the public: a great and unexpected success onstage, a film breaking all box-office records around the world, a dozen or more books on the best-seller lists for months, countless highly rated television documentaries, and, incredibly, at last count, an astonishing 9,866 separate entries on the Internet.

Her sinking, in the early hours of April 15, 1912, remains the quintessential disaster of the 20th century. A total of 1,517 souls—men, women and children—lost their lives. For the first time since the beginning of the Industrial Revolution early in the 19th century, bigger, stronger and grander did not automatically prove to be better. Suddenly the very essence of "progress" had to be questioned. Might the advancement of technology not always be progress? Royal Mail Steamer *Titanic* carried the dreams of a new era, one that had the people's complete faith that steam and steel and coal could create something stronger than nature. They were wrong.

Maury Yeston and Peter Stone

Nautical Bearings

The idea for turning this tremendous saga into a stage musical came to me some eight or nine years before it opened on Broadway (April 23, 1997). But the story of *Titanic* had, ever since I was a child, held a strong fascination for me. The part which gripped me most was the very concept of survival itself, and most particularly, *my* survival; had I actually been on that ship, would I have lived or died? I'd like to believe that I wouldn't have done anything dishonorable—one man aboard put a woman's shawl over his head in an attempt to secure a place in one of the "women and children only" lifeboats—but would I, as did *all* of the great millionaires in 1st Class, have stood stoically at the rail and died like a gentleman? Or would I, as some few passengers succeeded in doing after the last boats had pulled away, have found a way, any way, to avoid drowning in that freezing water? I've always believed I would.

But a musical? When I left California at seventeen to come to New York for the first time, so-called "book" musicals were in their infancy; *Oklahoma!* was still running, and soon followed by *Carousel*, *Annie Get Your Gun* and *Finian's Rainbow*. And while these were a far cry from the carefree musical comedies—collections of wonderful songs by the Gershwins, Cole Porter, Jerome Kern, Rodgers and Hart, and Irving Berlin that were glued together by rather simple libretti—that had earlier been the standard fare of the Twenties and Thirties, they were still, despite some rather dark elements in the best of them (death, crime, racism), pure entertainment.

Slowly, over the next four decades, musical comedy began to be replaced by musical theatre. Certainly there were, and continue to be, wonderfully and purely lighthearted shows that are among the best of America's home-grown art form—*Guys and Dolls*, *Kiss Me Kate*, *My Fair Lady*, *A Funny Thing Happened on the Way to the Forum*—but serious, even somber themes began to inject themselves into many of Broadway's biggest hits—*West Side Story*, *Fiddler on the Roof*, *Gypsy*, *Company*, *1776*, *Cabaret* and *A Chorus Line* to name only a few.

And then, in the Eighties and Nineties, mainly due to an influx of British and French "spectaculars" and, equally influential, the highly original works of Stephen Sondheim, musical theatre flirted with—and in some cases, embraced—*unhappy* endings.

> Many people wondered why I would want to do a "musical" about 1,500 people who died.

I have no particular objection to unhappy endings; but I see more dramatic benefit in following an unsettling climax with a hopeful, even optimistic denouement. Nothing could be sadder than the old King of Siam's death but it is followed by the inspirational elevation of the young and determined new king. As for *Titanic*, many people, including friends and family, wondered why I would want to do a "musical" about 1,500 people who died. But in the show Maury Yeston and I wrote, those deaths are not the end of the story; the lost are followed by the survivors, with their dreams and hopes and their memories of courage, sacrifice and, yes, survival, inspiring them, and, we hoped, us as well. That's what we intended the audience to be left with at the final curtain. We believe it is uplifting, the way theatre should be.

And there was something else that recommended this wonderful story. I had become interested in actual events as subjects for musical theatre when I wrote *1776* and, later, *The Will Rogers Follies*. The success of both encouraged me to look for yet other opportunities.

I have always believed, as a general rule, that nonfiction (i.e., history and/or reportage) is not compatible with the dramatic form. As a European playwright once put it: "God does not provide second acts." Historical stories provide good first acts, and often satisfying, even exciting, third acts; but that pesky *second* act, that most important of acts, in which the beginning leads invariably, immutably to its proper conclusion—or as critic Francis Fergusson defined it in his remarkable book, *The Idea of Theatre*, the Act of Passion that falls between the Act of Purpose and the Act of Perception—almost always, in nonfiction, turns out to be a prosaic, often puerile, and therefore theatrically unsuitable, entity. Either the facts must be changed to create dramatic unity and impact—thus corrupting truth—or the dramatic values must be sacrificed to maintain the historical integrity of the facts—thus creating, in most cases, tedium.

Captain Edward J. Smith

In *The Will Rogers Follies*, this problem was immediately evident in the mundane nature of Will's actual biography. In fact, the only event of real theatrical value in his life was the way he left it, the victim of an airplane crash in Alaska which cut him down in middle age. Then why bother to do his life at all? Because, while there was little drama or excitement in his personal life, the phenomenon of his public, professional life—what he said and what he accomplished, becoming the biggest, most beloved star this nation has ever produced, the number one box-office attraction in every single medium of his day (stage, films, radio, newspapers and the lecture circuit), was well worth dramatizing. The solution to this problem was in assigning to the great showman, Florenz Ziegfeld, whose lavish spectacles had headlined Rogers for ten years, the job of presenting Will's life as *he*, not God, would have conceived it. Thus the order and settings could be changed without altering the facts, so long as the facts were known.

But now and again, a true story will come along that's tailor-made for the stage. Courtroom drama (i.e., *Inherit the Wind*) and political debate (*1776*) are two forms that translate comfortably to the stage. And the ordeal of *Titanic* is certainly another: a chronicle that has become a universal legend, one which combines excitement, romance, tragedy, heroism, venality and sacrifice, one peopled with original and fascinating characters, its entire action satisfying the Aristotelian unities (occurring in one confined space during a proscribed period of time), and all of it engendered by an event so unlikely that, were it not true, wouldn't (and shouldn't) be believed by any audience: the unsinkable ship sinking on its maiden voyage. The greatest vessel ever constructed set sail and *never arrived anywhere*!

> Now and again, a true story will come along that's tailor-made for the stage.

One of the more fascinating aspects of dealing theatrically with history is the inspiring, in an audience, of that vital and necessary dramatic element known as "suspension of disbelief." This double negative (it's not the adoption of belief that's achieved, but the suspension of *dis*belief) defines one of the most remarkable things about theatre: the spectator's willing and eager participation in the experience.

We go to theatre, and especially the musical theatre, knowing full well it's not reality, that it is, in its many components, extremely artificial—lights, painted scenery, makeup, actors, singers, dancers, an orchestra—and all of it shared with total strangers sitting on all sides of us. But, because we all enjoy (require?) being told stories, and because we cannot enjoy them if we don't believe them, we willingly join in, thereby agreeing to a binding though unwritten contract between the storytellers and ourselves: we will believe despite *all* evidence to the contrary!

It is truly awe-inspiring to see and hear an audience "surprised" by developments they already know perfectly well. I have seen it at work at every performance of *1776*. They certainly know the Declaration of Independence was ratified and signed but they are in great, even agonizing suspense as the final vote draws near. They know Will Rogers will die in an air crash—we tell them at the beginning of the show—but they are shocked when it actually happens. And they surely know the *Titanic* will sink; but at every performance they gasp when they hear the news. And the best part is that the author need do nothing to achieve this wondrous effect; he has only to stand back and do nothing to prevent it. The audience will, and wants to, achieve it for themselves.

All of these ideas about this great true story rattled around in my mind for a year or two. Then, in 1990, as good fortune would have it, I was in Boston, called in, along with an old friend, composer-lyricist Maury Yeston, to rescue the musical *Grand Hotel*, which was threatened with closing before reaching Broadway. Right from the start of our collaboration Maury and I found a method of working that was mutually compatible. Collaboration among the creators of the three elements of a musical—book, music and lyrics—is a fragile thing, not unlike a marriage. First, it requires a method of working (more about that later). Second, it calls for a number of disciplines, some of them occasionally contradictory: tact and honesty, praise and criticism, patience and energy, being firm without being overbearing, and, above all, trust. And third, there must be the ability to relax and have a good time. Usually there are three persons involved, but when the composer and lyricist are rolled into one, like Sondheim, like Jerry Herman, and like Maury Yeston, there can be benefits—no ganging up, fewer misunderstandings—and dangers—no third person to referee. But luckily, Maury and I were compatible, both professionally and socially—we both tell terrible jokes—right from the start. We fully enjoyed that earlier collaboration and it apparently had a positive result: *Grand Hotel* ran over 1000 performances on Broadway.

During one of our moments of relaxation, Maury confessed to having a wonderful idea for a new musical: *Titanic*. Astonished, I admitted that I, too, had been harboring (so to speak) the same notion. Right then and there we agreed to write it together. Because of several other projects that involved us separately, however, it would take us six long years to get our show down on paper.

Titanic Undertakings

This might be a good moment to pause and reflect on why this country, and the entire world, has become fixated on the *Titanic* story. There are, of course, many reasons, not least of which is the fascination with the incredible event itself. But why now, after eighty-five years?

1st Class passenger John Jacob Astor

First, the discovery of the wreck rekindled the interest that had flared after Walter Lord's wonderful *A Night to Remember* hit the book best-seller lists four decades ago. Now, though, people could actually see the ship in the breathtaking undersea photos that accompanied the news stories.

There were those, of course, who raised their voices in protest at this late-20th century technological "grave-robbing" of the early century's hallowed ground. After all, there were attempts to raise not only artifacts, but whole sections of her steel hull. Personally, on reflection, I don't really find any desecration—to my mind the wreck of the *Titanic* is no more a "sacred tomb" than, say, a Florida trailer park destroyed by a hurricane—but I do have some qualms about the relentless commercialization of every lump of coal, every teaspoon and every chamber-pot that's brought to the surface. To my mind, it's unsettlingly similar to the vulgar selling fervor that followed the sad death of Princess Diana.

Another reason for the immense popularity of *Titanic* is, I believe, the approaching end of the century. The ship sank near the beginning of it, and now, at the end, we still consider the name *Titanic* a synonym for disaster, almost to the point where the word, lower case "t," cannot be used without conjuring up images of the ship.

> Another reason for the immense popularity of Titanic is the approaching end of the century.

And further, this has been the century of technology—from airplanes, automobiles, telephones, radio and television, to computers and landing men on the moon. Life on earth continues to change more rapidly each decade than in all of history combined. And in all of this progress, *Titanic* stands out as a warning that, as stated above, "progress" is not always progress.

Our Broadway show was to be followed, in some five or six months, by the motion picture—the most successful ever made—with the same title. I'm continually being asked, did the film help or hurt our musical? A little of both, perhaps; during the frenzy over the movie our box-office, too, enjoyed sharing the title and subject. When the film finally left the theatres (though the release of its millions of videocassettes again caused a tidal wave of interest), we suffered a momentary dip caused, no doubt, by consumer fatigue. But that turned out to be short-lived; business again picked up and the ship, quite happily, sails on.

Getting it afloat in the first place, however, was no day on the lake.

Long Hours in the Shipyard

The *Titanic* saga was a difficult one to synthesize—there were so many characters, so many facts and incidents, so many themes. But Maury and I moved forward with remarkable agreement and, yes, even a mystic sort of symbiosis whereby one of us would hit upon a new idea that the other would intuit even before hearing it. A lot of our early work was done over lunch in a small Chinese restaurant on Second Avenue and 70th Street—to the chagrin of the waiters who had to endure us occupying their tables until late in the afternoon. We even began grading the importance of our themes and characters by placing them in column A and column B. (The fortune cookies remained consistently optimistic.)

The first phase of our work was, of course, research. There are some eight or ten good books dealing with *Titanic*, but three or four were the most useful: Walter Lord's well-written and widely read *A Night to Remember* and his less-known but equally fascinating *The Night Lives On*, which deals with the aftermath of the tragedy. Another invaluable (and excellent) source was *The Maiden Voyage* by Geoffrey Marcus. And from a remainder table we found a book published only a few months after the actual event, *The Sinking of the Titanic and Great Sea Disasters*, which, though compiled too hurriedly to be constantly accurate, nevertheless provided great insight into the world of 1912.

But we were also fascinated by the complete transcripts of both the American and British official inquiries into the sinking. In fact, these interrogations were actually utilized, in the early versions of the show, as a method of transmitting information to the audience without having to seed it artfully into the dialogue. These inquiries were used, not as flashbacks, but rather as flash*forwards*, involving crew members called to testify about such things as the ship's speed, the iceberg warnings and the visibility on the fateful night as they simultaneously performed their shipboard duties, speaking, as it were, to the future as they behaved in the present. As the author, I was very enthusiastic about this device; I would, finally, give it up very reluctantly.

> A researcher was employed to organize the great ocean of facts.

A researcher was then employed to organize the great ocean of facts we had compiled into four looseleaf volumes, cross-indexed by date, by hour (and, on the fatal night, minute-by-minute), by character name, by logistic data, and by sociological import.

The conformation of the ship itself was remarkable. R.M.S. (Royal Mail Steamer) *Titanic* was constructed in Belfast, Ireland, in the great shipyards of Harland and Wolff. Her nine decks contained three separate libraries, a complete gymnasium, a squash court, a Turkish bath, a pitch-and-putt golf course and a 33-foot indoor bathing pool. She featured twenty-eight 1st Class Suites, variously decorated in Italian, Renaissance, Georgian, Regency, Queen Anne, Old Dutch, Louis XIV, XV and XVI, and Modern styles.

She was built at a cost of 1,500,000 pounds, was 882 feet long (standing on end she'd rise higher than the tallest skyscraper then in New York), and weighed 46,000 tons. Her great rudder alone weighed more (101 tons) than the entire *Santa Maria* (and she carried more saloon waiters than the entire crews of Columbus's three ships combined). Her 16 coal-burning boilers produced the steam that drove two reciprocating engines and one low-pressure turbine which, together, manufactured 66,000 horsepower. Only three of her four great funnels were functional, the rear stack being merely for aesthetic show. Her top speed was designed to be 23 knots, though, in actual operation, she never exceeded 22½.

Radioman Harold Bride

She carried enough provisions to supply a small town: 61 tons of meat, poultry and fish; 40 tons of potatoes; 36,000 apples and an equal number of oranges; 42,000 fresh eggs; 7,000 heads of lettuce; 1,500 gallons of milk; five tons of sugar; 37,000 bottles of wine, beer and spirits; 55,000 china dishes and 20,000 crystal drinking glasses; and 8,000 cigars.

Our next job was to translate as much of this information as we could into the language of musical theatre: both song lyrics and dialogue. "How did they build *Titanic*?" a crewman sings as the show begins:

> *Near a thousand feet in length*
> *Huge beyond past endeavor*
> *Strong beyond mortal strength*
> *Forty-six thousand tons of steel*
> *Eleven stories high*
> *She's a great palace, floating*
> *Quiet as a lullaby*

For Maury and myself, the providing of such information was a very important element of our musical. But even more important was the selection of the characters. Clearly we could not include, as the film did, 2,300 individuals; the practical (and financial) limitations of the stage allowed us only forty to fifty. And we were determined, also unlike the film, to include only *actual* persons; we would invent no one. But which to select?

As for the passengers: 1st Class (or 1st Cabin, as it was then called) was graced by almost every important American multi-millionaire—Astor, Guggenheim, Straus, Thayer, Widener and more—powerful men who, with their wives and families, were the regular and frequent passengers on the great transatlantic liners. Only Vanderbilt and Morgan missed the sailing, but both had booked, only at the last minute to cancel (Morgan because of ill health, and Vanderbilt because his wife's mother, who was accompanying them, didn't trust maiden voyages).

2nd Class was filled with merchants, professionals, tourists, many of them socially ambitious, wanting nothing more than participation in this glittering event. They had booked passage so they could rub up against the 1st Class; perhaps some of that golden charisma would even rub off.

In 3rd Class (commonly called steerage), there were the European emigrants leaving the old world, eager to reach the new. Irish, Turkish, Italian, Scandinavian —they were fleeing poverty and hopelessness, in search of opportunity and the gold the streets of America were purported to be paved with. Eating aboard the ship more and better food than they were accustomed to, they spent, for the first time in their lives, four full days in idleness. They had been assigned to *Titanic* by lottery and didn't really care which ship it was as long as it would get them to America.

And attending to all three classes (though admittedly more to 1st than to 3rd) were the officers and crew—more than 900 serving 1,400 passengers. The crew consisted of two kinds: seamen, who ran the ship, and, by far the largest group, the hotel staff, who managed the accommodations.

As we began the process of selecting our characters, a definite pattern emerged—our main characters would be presented in groups of three. The first trio we would meet are common

The full cast

seamen—Fred Barrett, a stoker who shoveled coal in boiler room #6; Harold Bride, a radioman who operated one of the earliest versions of the Marconi wireless telegraph; and Frederick Fleet, a young, green lookout who had never seen an iceberg in his entire life—each having first-hand knowledge of the three forces mentioned above (speed, ice and poor visibility), that would prove to be instrumental in destroying the ship.

Balancing them would be three *un*common men—J. Bruce Ismay, the owner; Thomas Andrews, the designer and builder; and E. J. Smith, the captain—each revealing a flaw of character: greed, compromise and compliance. Collectively they adhere to the Greek concept of a tragic figure. And when their faults collide with the ineluctable forces of nature, the ship's fate is sealed. In classical tragedy, this collision is inevitable. That it occurred in reality (and on the maiden voyage) was astounding. And now legendary.

And then we selected three emigrants in steerage—three young Irish girls, all named Kate— who are bound for a new life in America, a place very few from this class would survive to see. When we discovered these three poor girls on the passenger list, all traveling alone, and all with the same first name—as one of them remarks to a young man on board she's taken a

fancy to, "We're all named Kate, you know that"—we found them irresistible as characters.

From among the 2nd Class, we chose two composite couples: the Beanes and the Clarkes. The former, Edgar and Alice, a shopkeeper and his socially ambitious wife from the American Midwest; and the latter, Charles and Caroline, a young English couple, she of noble birth, he of the middle class, who are going to America where two people from different backgrounds can marry without interference from their strict, class-conscious parents, brazenly pretending to be already married in order to save the price of an extra cabin.

And representing the 1st Class, the five millionaires and their wives—John Jacob and Madeline Astor, Isador and Ida Straus, George and Eleanor Widener, John and Marion Thayer, and, accompanied by his mistress, Mme. Aubert, not his wife, Benjamin Guggenheim. And a mysterious widow, Mrs. Charlotte Cardoza, who had booked the most expensive suite on the ship and traveled with 15 steamer trunks and an additional three wooden crates containing 70 dresses, ten fur coats, 38 large feather pieces, 91 pairs of gloves, her personal pillows and sheets, plus a medicine chest and four little Pekinese dogs.

As for the officers and crew: besides Capt. Smith, we selected 1st Officer William Murdoch, 2nd Officer Charles Lightoller, 3rd Officer Herbert Pitman, 4th Officer Joseph Boxhall and Quartermaster Robert Hitchens. Murdoch was in command on the bridge when the collision occurred; it is commonly believed that he committed suicide just before the ship sank (he brooded that, had he had the presence of mind to ram the iceberg head-on, rather than sideswiping it in an attempt to avoid it altogether, he would have staved the bow, certainly lost a few lives, but the ship would have stayed afloat, saving the rest). Lightoller, the highest ranking officer who survived, was sucked into a ventilator when the ship went under; at the point of drowning, he was miraculously blown out by a great rush of air coming from the breached boilers and landed in the water beside a lifeboat where friendly hands pulled him in. (He went on to live a long, happy life, and, during World War Two, sailed his personal yacht to Dunkirk where, with his son, he participated in the historic evacuation of British troops.)

There were so many fascinating and colorful characters aboard *Titanic* that we found it terribly frustrating to leave any of them out. Even more upsetting were those whom we originally included and later, because of length, had to cut. Of these, by far the most compelling was Charles Joughin, Chief Baker, who worked in the ship's galley. Joughin, after learning that the ship was doomed, returned to his cabin to retrieve two bottles of good cognac (he had long enjoyed an intense thirst for distilled liquor). Then, loading a basket with freshly baked bread (and loading himself with most of the contents of one of his bottles), he proceeded to the Main Deck where he stocked each lifeboat with two of his loaves before the boat was launched. Then he joined the others who'd been left behind in struggling aft, toward the stern which was, by the minute, rising higher and higher out of the water. Finally, when the ship had attained a nearly vertical position, its stern a full 200 feet (20 stories) above the water, Joughin, having by now consumed both bottles, was still sufficiently conscious to realize that jumping from such a height would be suicidal. Climbing over the rear rail, he found himself standing next to the great rudder; a moment later, as *Titanic* began its fatal plunge, sliding straight down, rapidly, like an elevator, into the black sea, Charles Joughin not only rode her down, but managed to step off, into the water, at the very moment she disappeared beneath the surface. Incredibly, his head never got wet. More incredibly, while none of the hundreds of others in the water was able to survive the freezing (31 degrees) water for more than 20 or 30 minutes, Joughin managed to stay afloat for more than two full hours, a testament, no doubt, to the two fifths of French anti-freeze he'd consumed. He survived with no ill effects. Cutting this wonderful story was heartbreaking.

> One of the most important thematic decisions we made was to equate the three classes aboard the ship with the corresponding classes of Anglo-American society . . .

One of the most important thematic decisions we made was to equate the three classes aboard the ship (1st, 2nd and 3rd) with the corresponding classes of Anglo-American society (upper, middle and lower) as they existed at that time. When we discovered the discrepancy between the number of survivors from each of the ship's classes—all but two of the women in 1st Class were saved while 155 women and children from 2nd and 3rd (mostly 3rd) drowned—we understood why there was, following the accident, a new, long-overdue scrutiny of the prevailing class system and its values.

It is not an exaggeration to state that the 19th century, with its rigid social strictures, its extravagant codes of honor and sacrifice, and its unswerving belief that God favored the rich, also sank that night; it wasn't God who determined survival—it was man.

But it was God (or nature) who provided the iceberg. And that's a major reason why this story has so strongly resonated over the past eighty-five years: the fascination readers and audiences display for natural disasters such as earthquakes, twisters and hurricanes, tidal waves, meteors, volcanos, and, yes, as in the case of *Titanic*, even icebergs.

The reason for this attraction is, I believe, a desire on the part of us human beings to recognize and reaffirm our place in the cosmic order of things, and to find, not only consolation, but solace in it. How comforting it is to know that no matter how high man rises, how Godlike his achievements, that he is subject to the same natural laws that encompass the rest of nature. What a load off our backs, what a relief to know that we're *not* gods! Which is why, as novelist John Updike wrote, nothing devised by man is unsinkable.

So with our themes and characters set, our next move was to establish the tone. Act One could be completely carefree; this was, after all, the maiden voyage of the largest, strongest and safest ship in history, thereby allowing a liberal amount of humor, most of it resulting from the behavior of the upper and middle classes: the soon-to-be antediluvian social mores of the former and the relentless ambitions of the latter.

But Act Two would be quite the opposite— a tense progression among both the passengers and crew from denial, to doubt, to realization, to acceptance, then on to horror, panic and, finally, despair as the extent of the catastrophe became more and more evident.

High Seas Dramatization

With all these elements in hand, we could now begin to work out the action. Here was the story we wanted to tell: *Titanic* set sail on her maiden voyage from Southampton, England, on April 10, 1912. After stops in Cherbourg, France, and Queenstown (now Cobh), Ireland, she headed west, across the North Atlantic. During the first four carefree days the passengers in every class were enjoying an uncommonly smooth crossing and were growing increasingly eager for their arrival in New York. On the bridge, the officers were experiencing a faultless voyage; the new ship was behaving perfectly. True, there were warnings from several other ships in the vicinity of ice fields and large bergs straying farther south than normal for that time of the year, but there seemed to be little if any concern. After all, what could happen to such a ship? Wasn't she constructed with sixteen watertight compartments that could be mechanically closed off in the unlikely case of a breach?

True, the managing director of the White Star Line, J. Bruce Ismay, the son of the line's founder, was making a pest of himself, continually hectoring the Captain to increase speed—he wanted a record for this maiden voyage, the publicity of which would help recapture some of the luster (and business) lost to the rival Cunard ships.

And, true, the Captain, E. J. Smith, the acknowledged "Commodore" of the North Atlantic, having recently retired after four distinguished decades at sea with service aboard no less than seventeen separate White Star ships, was pressured to return and command this prestigious maiden voyage. He wearily bowed to his employer's pressure and raised the ship's speed near to its maximum—22½ knots.

And also true, the builder of the ship, Thomas Andrews, aboard his creation for this pre-

Brian d'Arcy James (Frederick Barrett, Stoker) and Martin Moran (Harold Bride, Radioman)

The three Kates head the cast in a benefit performance in New York City.

miere crossing, had designed the watertight bulkheads to rise only as high as "C" deck, thereby providing the 1st Class passengers above with roomier accommodations, a compromise that would prove to be disastrous.

With these displays of negligence and of casting prudence overboard, the spectacular, enormous stage that was *Titanic* was set for tragedy.

At 11:40 P.M. on Sunday, April 14, the sea was calm, the night moonless, the air a degree above freezing, the water a degree below. The lookout spotted the massive iceberg a little too late—the customary binoculars were inexplicably missing from the crow's nest—and the ship reacted to his alarm a little too slowly. The berg scraped the starboard side of the ship beneath the waterline, slicing her open like a tin of sardines, dealing her, as we now know, a series of

six sliver-thin slits, breaching six of the watertight compartments. The ship was at that moment doomed. She could stay afloat with any three compartments flooded, perhaps even four; but certainly not six. In less than two and a half hours she would sink.

The passengers, especially those in 1st Class, many of whom had not even felt the impact, refused, at first, to believe there was any danger. (Those in steerage knew there was trouble—the water was pouring into their dormitory cabins.) But as the ship began to list more and more severely, it was no longer possible to deny the inevitable.

There were only twenty lifeboats. To accommodate every soul aboard, there should have been fifty-four, but that many would have taken away too much deck space from 1st Class. Even so, the first couple of boats were lowered nearly empty—who in their right mind could leave the large, warm, brightly lit, "unsinkable" leviathan for a tiny open boat bobbing about in the pitch black night and the freezing cold sea in the middle of the vast Atlantic Ocean?

Finally, when the last of these boats had departed, there were still over fifteen hundred souls left aboard, including every last one of the American millionaires (and the wife of one, Isador Straus, the owner of Macy's, who after forty-one years of marriage, refused to leave her husband's side).

When the end finally came, when the stern of the great ship rose high above the ocean's surface and she stood that way, on end, almost perpendicular, for a few brief moments, with over a thousand screaming people desperately, hopelessly clinging to it, she at last surrendered to her injuries and plunged straight down to her grave.

In a matter of seconds THE LARGEST MOVING OBJECT ON EARTH HAD TOTALLY DISAPPEARED.

And going down with her: an original, jewel-encrusted copy of *The Rubaiyat of Omar Khayyam*, a safe containing $850,000 in cash and $5,000,000 worth of diamonds, seven grand pianos, the ultramodern 50-phone switchboard, a case of gloves for Marshal Field in

Philadelphia, 30 cases of assorted golf clubs and tennis rackets, a magnificent silver duck press, and a great measure of the optimism, self-confidence and complacency of the English-speaking world that technology would bring them heaven on earth.

Fifty bellboys, none more than 15 years old, would die without a whimper. Seventy-six of the 84 stokers and all 38 engineers would perish in the act of providing heat and electricity up to the very end. Thirty-seven dogs, 11 cats and a pet pig went down with the ship. Of the 2,228 human beings aboard, only 711 survived.

And the band played on, to the very end.

Builder Thomas Andrews

Ordering all of this into an extremely detailed outline, Maury and I finally sat down to create the script and score. Our method of working was devised from our own past experiences. For my part, I had written musical books to already completed scores, and I had also done the reverse, completing the book before the composer and lyricist began to work. But by far the most efficacious method had been to work simultaneously, none of us allowed to get ahead of the others, fleshing out each scene and finding, together, those moments to musicalize. And that's precisely the way we proceeded. Several months later, after very little disagreement, we had a completed first draft with, coincidentally, 27 scenes and 27 musical numbers.

During this period of close cooperation we discovered a form neither of us had ever used, nor, in fact, ever seen: I would write a scene (on the bridge, for instance, a dialogue between the captain and his officers) and then Maury would take certain key sentences, even entire exchanges, and set them to music, to be sung, while an ever-present underscoring would maintain an actual melody into which the sung phrases would precisely fit, yet all the while leaving large portions of it to be spoken. This form resembled in some ways the *recitativo* found in opera, but with the difference that the singing and dialogue were mixed together. We were able to use this complex but totally fluid device many times within the show, and, we believe, to great effect.

Neither the subject nor placement of the actual songs was hard to find. Barrett, the young British stoker, would sing of his desire to go to sea to escape the coal mines of Leicestershire only to find himself, ironically, still shoveling coal, this time deep below the waterline of a ship ("Barrett's Song"). Bride, the radioman, would sing of how, as a young man, he'd spent most of his time alone, shy of relationships, but having discovered Marconi's radio, he could now boldly converse with the entire world ("The Night Was Alive"). And Fleet, the lookout, in his crow's nest high atop the ship, would anxiously remark on the conditions of the flat calm sea, the dark and moonless sky, and the cold and windless air ("No Moon").

Capt. Smith, Bruce Ismay and Thomas Andrews, who, when we first meet them in Act

One, will sing their own, self-satisfied praises over having presented the world with a marvel such as *Titanic* ("The Largest Moving Object"}, would then, in Act Two, when the fate of the ship has been confirmed, sing of the accountability they angrily assign to each other ("The Blame").

In 1st Class, the millionaires and their ladies could smugly reflect on their privileges while sitting at the Captain's table ("What a Remarkable Age This Is"), while in 3rd Class, the three Irish girls named Kate would sing of their deepest, dearest desires to go to the New World where they'll be able to rise far above their mean, hard lives back home, achieving goals hardly even dreamt of ("Ladies Maid").

And in 2nd Class, Edgar and Alice Beane would spend their time bickering over her desire to "rub elbows" with the swells in 1st Class, even though such access is barred by the rules of the ship, and his determination to keep her from embarrassing herself. Finally, boldly sneaking into a lively and spirited *the-dansant* on "A" Deck—held on Sunday afternoon, mere hours before the collision, it is the last joyful and carefree moment of the voyage ("Doing the Latest Rag")—she will then sing of her heady experience when she's later confronted by her husband ("I Have Danced").

In Act Two, the tone and subjects of the songs would, perforce, have to change. Beginning with the arousing of the still-unsuspecting passengers in all three of the ship's classes ("Wake Up, Wake Up"), to their awkward gathering in the public rooms ("Dressed in Your Pyjamas in the Grand Salon"), the 3rd Class where the emigrants find themselves barred from ascend-

David Garrison (J. Bruce Ismay), John Cunningham (Capt. E. J. Smith) and Michael Cerveris (Thomas Andrews)

ing to the lifeboat deck ("The Staircase"), to the plaintive, heartbreaking avowal by all of the husbands remaining aboard to their wives in the lifeboats below ("We'll Meet Tomorrow"), the progressing moods of the ship's company, from complacence to despair, must be displayed.

After the last lifeboat has pulled away from the ship, those left aboard are resigned to their fate. The elderly Strauses, Isador and Ida, who, because of her courageous and loving self-sacrifice, will be spending what short time is left of their lives together, standing at the rail of the seriously listing liner, singing of their mutual devotion ("Still").

Only Thomas Andrews, the designer of *Titanic*, alone in the 1st Class smoke room, appears oblivious to his own fate. Poring over a set of the ship's plans, he somehow, in his oncoming madness, resolves to correct, then and there, her faulty design, thereby saving it. But as the ship lists more and more acutely, and with the furniture and loose objects

Larry Keith (Isador Straus) and Alma Cuervo (Ida Straus)

tumbling and careening around him, he will suddenly be jolted back to his senses and sing, with glaring insight of what is about to befall his creation ("Mr. Andrews' Vision").

The several scenes inhabited by most, if not all, of the cast, would become extremely complicated musical constructions of themes, melodies, counter-melodies and their variations. The scene depicting the loading and sailing of the great ship, which would open the show, was finally given over, with only a few spoken lines of dialogue, entirely to singing, beginning with the crew's first sighting of the ship ("There She Is") and ending as she leaves the dock ("Godspeed *Titanic*").

At the end of Act One, a cross-section of the ship, from the bridge and crow's nest above, down through the 1st, 2nd and 3rd Class decks, to a game of cards in the smoke room, will feature the passengers and crew as they express their hopes and plans after landing in New York. This equally complex scene would combine both speaking and singing, but without using any specific song—except for Yeston's version of an air called "Autumn," performed by the ship's orchestra, which harked back to an earlier composition by that name which was, contrary to the prevailing myth, the one actually played by the ship's orchestra as *Titanic* sank (and not "Nearer My God to Thee").

But it was the scene depicting the loading and lowering of the lifeboats that presented, by far, the most difficult problem for musicalization. Maury and I came up with at least a half dozen of what we thought were solutions, but none of them was wholly satisfying. Spoken, the scene was too cinematic for the stage; when speech and song were alternated, the effect, in this particular scene, was awkward and disjointed, robbing the moment of its obligatory emotion. Finally, near the end of our rehearsal period, just prior to previews, Maury would come up with an entirely sung version, again using many of the phrases and exchanges from the spoken scene, that, considering the abundance of incident to be covered, miraculously solved our dilemma.

And speaking of speaking: given our determination to deal only with actual events and characters, was the dialogue I created also historically accurate? It's a fair question. Since nearly all of the talk aboard the ship was never recorded—there are several notable exceptions, among them the Strauses declarations to each other which were reported by one of their servants who survived—the author's job was to attempt a *re-creation* of what must have been said, given the information available about the people and their circumstances. Very much like in *1776*, where, because the secretary of the Congress kept no minutes, dialogue and argument had to be reconstructed from the writings by and/or about the principal characters, that process was followed in *Titanic*.

Titanic's Brand-New Crew

With the script and score now in place, we were ready to proceed to the next stage: selecting a director. Because of the scope and size of the drama, we turned to a young Englishman who had mainly been involved with opera all over the world (he had recently mounted a controversial but widely-praised production of Wagner's complete "Ring Cycle" at London's Covent Garden) but who also had experience with a musical on London's West End—Stephen Sondheim and James Lapine's *Into the Woods* to which he gave a totally new interpretation and a Broadway play in New York—David Hirson's verse drama, *La Bête*, one of the most imaginative and creative productions I'd ever seen.

Richard Jones turned out to be a wise choice. He was unintimidated by the daunting assignment of recreating so large an event on the stage; he never once wavered in his concept, design or commitment. Further, his instinct for selecting actors is phenomenal and his total concentration is awesome. Further still, his experience in opera provided him with not only the ear but the method for dealing with our particular brand of *recitativo* (described above). Under his strong guidance we engaged the finest group of actor-singers (or were they singer-actors?) it has ever been our pleasure to work with. And he molded them into a tight, perfectly seamless company.

With the director on board, we began looking for a producer. Musicals based on films, plays or books are usually initiated by producers, but original ideas are almost always written before one is selected. Because word of our show had gotten around we were approached by one major entrepreneur who seemed extremely anxious to present it, not only on Broadway, but around the world. But after he read it, he circulated eight single-spaced pages of what we first thought were suggestions, but which turned out to be a list of requirements. The first was an instruction to change the title; "Nothing called "*Titanic*" can possibly succeed," he wrote. That producer quickly sank from sight.

In 1996, still looking for a producer who didn't mind using *Titanic* as a title, we took our show to an energetic, relatively new producing team known more for their successful musical revivals (*Guys and Dolls, The King and I*) than any original shows, but their productions were all well-mounted and -maintained. The Dodgers (named for the baseball team they all followed in Brooklyn when the three partners—Michael David, Ed Strong and Sherman Warner—were young) gave it not only their unstinting devotion but their lavish financial support as well. Their commitment, like Richard Jones', was, and remains, total.

Richard demanded a workshop several months before rehearsals were scheduled to begin, with only twelve actors, six men and six women (each of whom played several characters irrespective of age or sex) to give him a sense of the dramatic progression of the scenes and the physical movement of the characters. It was just prior to this time that Richard argued against my concept of the simultaneous inquiries which were, in the early scripts, conducted by an offstage, unseen interrogator. He strongly maintained that the dispassionate collecting of factual testimony would interfere, and thereby weaken, the dramatic power achieved by allowing our characters to maintain, uninterrupted, their poignant and intense emotional involvements with one another. I'm still not sure if he convinced me or simply, with his fervent, unceasing conviction, wore me down. In any case, the inquiries went. But I continue to think of them and I still wonder.

As our scenic designer, Richard recommended (and we readily agreed) a collaborator of his from the opera, Stewart Laing, a redheaded Scotsman with a heavy (often impenetrable) brogue, who would create both the complicated sets and the lavish period costumes. Stewart turned out to be the perfect choice. Attempting to present a spectacle the size of *Titanic* within the confines and limitations of a Broadway playhouse demanded, not only an impressionistic concept, but an engineering miracle. We were determined to show the ship actually sinking on stage—and Stewart's success in creating this mechanical marvel has been cheered at every performance.

To round out the design team we selected two Broadway veterans: lighting designer Paul Gallo and sound designer Steve Canyon Kennedy. And finally, as our orchestrator, we chose Jonathan Tunick, the master veteran of seven Sondheim musicals, and for our musical director, Kevin Stites, who came to us from national companies of *Phantom of the Opera* and *Les Misérables*.

The only step left for us before rehearsals could begin was to select a choreographer. Here there was much disagreement: should he or she be an old Broadway hand, or, considering there was not much in the way of standard musical dancing in our show (aside from the one motivated danced number, "The Latest Rag"), someone with a less formulaic approach?

Maury and I flew to Chicago to meet with Lynne Taylor-Corbett, an experienced chore-ographer but one with few Broadway credits. She was there working on Randy Newman's musical, *Faust*, and during a break we sat with her and talked. When it was time for Maury and me to return to New York she'd convinced us that she was the right person for the job. We were now ready for production.

Full Steam Ahead

Rehearsals, with our full complement of forty actors, began the day after the New Year's holi-day, 1997, in rented studio space on lower Broadway. There were the usual cuts (shows are always, in their early lives, too long), refinements or replacements of both songs and scenes, none of them overly traumatic (except for the aforementioned inquiries), and a constant examination of the show's running order to assure that its energy and tension progressed in a straight line.

There was a ballad sung by Caroline and Charles Clarke ("I Give You My Hand"), that was replaced by another ("I Will Love You"), then, after returning to the original, we tried out a third ("Social Class")—until, finally, we realized it wasn't the song that was causing us trouble, but the moment itself. We decided that there was only so much time to be spent with the 2nd Class passengers and that Alice and Edgar Beane were more valuable representa-tives of that group. The Clarkes' song was therefore cut, much to the understandable con-

A game of cards in the smoke room.

sternation of the actors (they were both hired for their fine singing voices) and to the composer, who'd written not one but three lovely melodies.

Another element of the show was closely watched during the rehearsal period: the maintenance of the audience's anxiety. Of course they knew about the impending disaster; but it would have been not only foolish to pretend they didn't, but irresponsible dramatically to ignore such a tension. We therefore kept a tight watch on this factor, satisfying ourselves that iceberg warnings, demands for more speed and other telltale signs of the impending disaster were sewn into the otherwise carefree fabric of the first act.

Toward this end I asked that a form of "running clock" be included in the scenic design. I had used this device to great advantage in a film I'd written some years before (*The Taking of Pelham One Two Three*) and recognized its effect on an audience's emotions. I also used it in the stage and film productions of *1776*, though in that play it would be fairer to call it a "running calendar," in which tension was created by having the pages of a wall calendar torn off as the fateful date (July 4th) grew nearer and nearer.

Don Stephenson (Charles Clark) and Judith Blazer (Caroline Neville)

In *Titanic* we used electronic L.E.D. displays on both sides of the proscenium arch to announce not only the date and time but, in many scenes, the ship's actual location. This device not only presaged the collision with the iceberg at the end of Act One, but accentuated the tension—for the audience, of course, but also for the characters onstage.

In early March we finally moved into our theatre, the Lunt-Fontanne on West 46th Street, for what was to be an intense and exhausting process known as "the tech"—the working out of all technical problems involved with the sets, lighting, sound, props, costumes, orchestrations and the other attendant elements, first making sure that each was what we foresaw, then making sure that it worked properly, and then, that each fit stylistically and seamlessly into the whole. This slow, painstaking and often stultifyingly tedious procedure can take days, even a week to complete; in our case, due to the hydraulic engineering that would create the illusion of the foundering ocean liner, it took nearly *two*—roughly the same amount of time the round-trip of the *Titanic* was expected to consume.

It must be noted here, because of the press frenzy that was soon to take place, that the engineering of the show never faltered, *not once!* It worked perfectly, from day one, and continues, as of this writing (the show being well into its second year on Broadway), to work perfectly eight times a week, a near-miraculous achievement.

Because of this technical complexity, and in no small part the horrific expenses involved in moving and supporting so many onstage and backstage people—at least 75—to say nothing of the mountain of equipment, the production was not able to travel. This ruled out the possibility of an any out-of-town try-out. *Titanic* was my fourteenth Broadway show and twelve of them had made this ritual hegira to a major city in the eastern half of the country for a trial run with a real, live audience. Boston, Washington, Toronto, Philadelphia, Baltimore or Detroit— they were the usual stops—were all just far enough from Broadway to discourage the masses of New York theatre people and journalists who were dying to know whether or not the show was a flop, from making the trip. As a result, the creative collaborators could work in relative privacy, listening to the audience reaction (an aggregate audience is almost always right) and, through their collective experience and instinct, translate that reaction into changes that will improve the show.

And sometimes those changes can be massive; entire acts have been scrapped; songs have been dropped, moved, rewritten or replaced; new scenes have been added and old ones reconceived; the running order has been revamped and rearranged; actors have been fired and new ones hired. All of these paroxysms are possible because out-of-town audiences are, for the most part, aware that the show is a work in progress and they are willing to be patient, understanding and cooperative because they sincerely wish you well.

> There is, unhappily, a very large contingent of the New York theatre people and journalists who pray *devoutly*, with all of their being, that any new show is a disaster.

But to skip this highly productive out-of-town process, to begin by previewing the show in New York, can be a deadly and often fatal experience. Because there is, unhappily, a very large contingent of the New York theatre people and journalists, mentioned above, who pray *devoutly*, with all of their being, that any new show is a disaster. And in the case of *Titanic*, a title synonymous with disaster, this malevolent hope reached new heights—or plumbed new depths, depending on whether you're rooting for the passengers or the sharks.

The motives of these two groups are totally different. The press wants a flop because it's more amusing and provocative to write about. Of all the hundreds of truly clever lines that have been printed and broadcast about Broadway plays and musicals over the past 75 years, *not one of them* was in praise of the show. And since most journalists who write about the arts are looking to make a name and career for themselves, the need to be amusing is irresistible.

But by far the more hurtful and upsetting ritual is the delight of our peers in being destructive. The Germans have a word for it—*schadenfreude*—which, roughly translated, means "malicious joy." It's not enough that your friends shouldn't succeed, they have to fail miserably. Over the years I have watched this poisonous thing happen; I have even, shamefully, felt the temptation to partake myself. I really can't explain it; after all, it's a proven theatrical truth that success breeds success, that it increases the public interest and helps us all. A rising tide lifts all boats, etc. etc. And yet, there they all are, preferably at the first preview because that's when the show will be seen to its greatest disadvantage. And then the word goes out, the jungle drums beat out their joyful message: "The show is in deep trouble!" Smiles and snickers all around. Why? I honestly don't know. It's enough to say that it's one of the saddest aspects of working in the Broadway theatre.

Matthew Bennett (Thomas Andrews in the show) with Production Supervisor Susan Green.

Rough Seas

And to make our lives even more complicated, our "tech" rehearsals, as I mentioned, lasted several days longer than anticipated. As a result we were forced to cancel our first three paid previews. This is a rather common occurrence out-of-town—if the show isn't ready for an audience, there can be no other choice. (And especially an audience as sophisticated as those attending a first New York preview.) This delay, however, caused the tabloid drama desks and columnists, and therefore the theatre cognoscenti, to hope that our stage machinery had failed us so they could jump in with both feet, which they did: "'*TITANIC*' REFUSES TO LEAVE PORT" and "THIS '*TITANIC*' WON'T SINK" were among the friskier of the mean-spirited headlines.

The actual trouble we were experiencing concerned a device in the Second Act that we had cut. The show had been scenically conceived to include five tableaux consisting of scale models. The first—*Titanic* steaming her way across a mirror-smooth sea, her lights blazing, her funnels smoking, oblivious of the iceberg which lies immediately ahead—closes the First Act and turned out to be one of the most breathtaking effects ever seen on a stage, equal, in our minds, to the helicopter in *Miss Saigon* and the chandelier in *Phantom of the Opera*.

But the remaining four models turned out to be less successful, and not always for the same reason. Two of them did not turn out to be as impressive as they promised to be on paper. A third was too difficult to achieve in the relatively short time we had to work it out. And the fifth and last, which was to end the show, was cut when the ending was reconceived.

It was the removal of one of these tableaux, halfway through the Second Act, which forced a scenic change that, of course, had not been anticipated, one that required a full *six minutes* to complete. But we had, for the moment, nothing to replace it with; there was, unavoidably, a six-minute gap. And in the theatre, six minutes of waiting in the dark is an eternity. Our only solution, until a replacement scene could be written, directed and orchestrated, was to have our stage manager announce, before the beginning of Act Two, that a pause in the action would be occurring. Naturally, this would only increase the feeding frenzy of the press.

This replacement scene, one of four major revisions accomplished during the four-week preview period, turned out to be another of those happy accidents that result, even (or especially) under pressure, in the invention of something that would be, not only a stop-gap (literally) solution, but a strong, positive improvement to the show.

The problem was further complicated by a scenic problem: we didn't have a set for a new scene. Normally, transitional scenes (and that's what this one would have to be) were played "down in one"—that is, a place far downstage, closest to the audience. (This area is known as "one," mid-stage is "two," and the full stage is "three.") But at this particular point in Act Two the great ship had already begun to list and all of the other sets were reflecting this. The flat, level downstage area, therefore, was ruled out.

And then we realized that we did have one painted drop of the outside hull of the listing *Titanic* which contained a slanting row of portholes, four of them practical. By placing plat-

> In the theatre, six minutes of waiting in the dark is an eternity.

forms of graduating heights behind these openings we could accommodate four actors, with only their heads showing. The set had originally been designed for a scene where the Captain went to the radio room after the lifeboats had been launched, to inquire if any ships were near enough to rescue the people stranded aboard, but this scene had only recently been cut, the same material having been covered elsewhere. But that scene had been barely two minutes long; how could four static talking heads remain interesting for *six*?

I was sitting in the theatre during an afternoon rehearsal pondering our predicament when an idea came. We had, the day before, made another one of the four major preview changes in the show, this one the deletion of one of the strongest songs Maury had written. Late in Act Two, on the severely slanting Main Deck, four millionaires—Astor, Guggenheim, Thayer and Widener—were discovered standing at the rail, dressed in their finest evening clothes, each with a silver flask of brandy, stoically awaiting death. In a short scene which had them searching for the justice in their hopeless situation, Guggenheim recalled a passage from a Balzac novel: "Behind every great fortune lies a great crime." Months before, when Maury and I were discussing song ideas, I had given him this quote and it inspired him to write a song ("Behind Every Fortune") which had the millionaires, about to die, confessing their crimes. Our director thought it was the finest song in the score and yet, he saw, when played before an audience, that it was an intellectual lyric coming at a time when an emotional one was needed. And, since the highly emotional duet sung by the elderly Strauses ("Still") came immediately after, the millionaires' song not only set the wrong tone, but lessened the impact of the subsequent moment. To everyone's sorrow, the brilliant but unwelcome millionaires' song was cut.

My new idea, then, was to resuscitate the millionaires' *scene*, which had also been cut, that ended with the Balzac quote, by placing them behind the four portholes. As this scene was no more than two minutes in length, I contrived that the millionaires would then step back, out of the light, and their places would be taken by four more of the stranded characters we knew: the two 2nd Class passengers, Edgar Beane and Charles Clarke, an infamous cardsharp, Jay Yates, who worked the Atlantic liners, and Fred Barrett, the young stoker, all of whom would reflect on their common fate. Another two minutes taken care of. Finally, these four would also step aside to allow four of the ship's personnel to take their places: Capt. Smith, 1st Officer Murdoch, Chief Steward Etches, a highly visible (and audible) character throughout the entire show, and a young (14) bellboy who constantly, in bad times as well as good, displayed a remarkably sunny disposition. This last group would reflect on both the past and on what might have been. When the Chief Steward, left alone at one of the portholes, ended the entire sequence with a fragment of a song originally sung by Murdoch in Act One ("To Be a Captain"), we finally had our six minutes!

The first time this cobbled new scene was performed we all stood at the back of the theatre praying it would hold the audience's attention. But none of us was prepared for the reaction—ours as well as theirs—it received. The twelve framed heads seen through the portholes, when lighted by Paul Gallo, looked amazingly like old Daguerreotypes, and when, four at a time, the characters stepped back out of the light, it was as if they were disappearing into the ether of the legend they'd all become part of. The audience sat in total silence (always, except in a comedy, a good sign) and it was clear they were deeply affected. In short, what started out to be merely a practical solution to a technical problem, turned out to be, in every way, a great asset to our show.

Our third preview fix was the quickest and easiest, but no less important to the show; it involved the 2nd Class couple, Edgar and Alice Beane. Having downplayed the Clarkes in their favor, we now, in previews, saw clearly that the Beanes needed an additional musical moment. Maury and I selected a short scene late in the 1st Act where the socially ambitious Alice, fresh from having sneaked onto the 1st Class deck where she actually danced with some of the millionaires, encounters her husband and, still flushed from the heady experience, shares with him her triumphal feelings. But his reaction is far less than she had hoped; a simple man, her pretensions are too extravagant for him. The scene ends with her desire to be alone, to think about the rest of their life together.

Sitting in the lounge of the theatre (a great deal of work is always done in the various lounges), Maury and I broke up the scene into sung and spoken sections. He then, on the spot, constructed a regular theatre song—two choruses, a release, and a final chorus—each segment of which to be separated by dialogue. It turned out to be a perfect blend of the two forms of expression and we were very proud of it, not least because, time being in short supply, we had done it so quickly and with no missteps. But more important, it again turned out to be a valuable contribution to the show.

But our biggest problem by far was how to end the story. Of course the ship would sink, but following that exciting and emotional climax, what would be exactly the right denouement to present to the audience, the best culmination of the drama they'd spent the preceding two and a half hours with?

I had earlier written a scene that presented some sixteen survivors, following their rescue by the steamer *Carpathia*, appearing in a line, on a bare stage, in front of a black curtain, expressing, one by one, their memories and innermost feelings following the sinking, speaking as much to the audience as to each other. Then, appearing at the end of this line, dressed in a modern, bright, anachronistic orange jumpsuit, a contemporary character would enter: Robert D. Ballard, a scientist from the Woods Hole Oceanographic Institution, who, on September 1, 1985, at a depth of two and a half miles below the ocean's surface, had been the first human being in 73 years to cast eyes on R.M.S. *Titanic*.

After describing his remarkable discovery, the curtain would then rise on the event itself— a tableau of Ballard's submersible, in miniature, of course, descending to the wreck of the great ship on the ocean's bottom. As stated earlier, this effect had turned out to be unsuccessful. But even if it had worked to our satisfaction, the moment itself was too dark, too impersonal and, most of all, too thematically inconclusive to serve as our ending.

A mere two weeks before opening night, then, we were without a satisfactory conclusion to the show. Adding to this dilemma was a further complication: the authors, the producers and the director, for one of the few times during our collaboration, were not in

> A mere two weeks before opening night, we were without a satisfactory conclusion.

mutual agreement as to the solution. Maury had written a fine song ("In Every Age") which he intended as a statement at the end of the show, but during rehearsals, it was decided that the song actually belonged at the very beginning, sung by Thomas Andrews, the designer of *Titanic*, as a comment on man's monumental creations sullied by his overreaching ambition and pride. But we also intended the song to be reprised by the line of survivors at the end. Our disagreement concerned whether they would only sing the song or perform both the scene and the song together.

Whichever idea prevailed, it was mutually acknowledged that this bleak line of speaking and/or singing survivors could not, of itself, end the show. There must be a full-stage moment, a larger statement of attainment, realization and fulfillment.

It's a testament to what had become our mutuality of vision that Richard Jones, Maury and I all came up with precisely the same idea at the same time: when the sixteen survivors, each clutching a gray wool blanket marked CARPATHIA around them, completed their scene and/or song (we still hadn't solved that one yet), the curtain behind them would rise to reveal the identical setting used at the opening of Act One—the great gangway, emblazoned with the words WHITE STAR LINE, leading up and off to the unseen *Titanic*, the entire scene bathed in bright morning sunlight. And there, scattered about the stage, in frozen positions, were all those who'd lost their lives. The survivors would then go to them, the living joining the dead—wives and husbands, friends and families, officers and crew—and they would stand and sing together a reprise of the uplifting song they sang as the ship first left its Southampton dock ("Godspeed *Titanic*") at the beginning of the show. Our faith in this ending was unanimous.

When we instructed the stage crew to work out the scenic change behind the survivors' black curtain—removing the tilting deck of the ship (the previous scene), and setting up the gangway—we received what seemed distressing news: it would take six full minutes (again six minutes!) to manage the change. But again, this magic number worked in our favor; our argument had been settled for us as we were now forced to use both the scene *and* the song in order to fill the time. And after only one performance before a preview audience we knew we had reached, regardless of the circuitous route, our home port.

So at last, with six days left before opening night (and only three before the first authorized appearance of the print critics) we'd finally completed our show. We were all quite satisfied that we had done everything we could to produce the work we'd envisioned.

What we could not have known, or even suspected, was that the press, from the very beginning, was quite hostile to the very idea of a musical based on a major maritime tragedy, especially the most noted shipwreck of the 20th Century. They were not only lying in wait, they were also drooling over the possibilities of greeting the show with such stored-up gems as: "*TITANIC* HITS ANOTHER ICEBERG!" and "*TITANIC* SINKS WITHOUT A TRACE!" and (my favorite) "ALL SINGING, ALL DANCING, ALL DROWNING!"

Riding High

Imagine their disappointment when, on opening night, they were unable to use these head-lines. They were forced to admit, many of them grudgingly, that the show was not the disas-ter they had so eagerly anticipated, that it was, in fact, a serious, important and artistically satisfying addition to that or any other Broadway season. As the critic for *The New Yorker* wrote:

> It seemed a foregone conclusion that [*Titanic*] would be a failure; a musical about history's most tragic maiden voyage, in which fifteen hundred people lost their lives, was obviously preposterous—as doomed as the ship itself. . . . But rumors of its sinking turn out to be greatly exagger-ated; a whole flotilla of maritime-disaster metaphors that were ready for active duty will have to remain tied up at the dock. . . . Astonishingly, *Titanic* manages to be grave and entertaining, somber and joyful; little by little you realize that you are in the presence of a genuine addition to American musical theatre.

Interestingly, there was not a single review, newspaper, magazine, television or radio, that did not mention, in its opening paragraphs, the "technical difficulties" that had, in fact, never occurred, regardless that such gossip, even if true, has no relevance whatsoever to a critic's opin-ion of the finished work.

Becky Ann Baker (Charlotte Cardoza), David Garrison (J. Bruce Ismay) and Andy Taylor (J. H. Rogers)

Then, a week after its opening, *Titanic* received five Tony Award nominations, and four weeks later, at the lavish Tony ceremony presented at Radio City Music Hall, *Titanic* achieved a record by winning *all five* of its nominated awards: Best Musical, Best Book, Best Score, Best Orchestrations and, ironically, Best Scenic Design.

From that night forward, *Titanic* has continued to sail on smoothly (as of this writing it's halfway through its second year on Broadway), setting house records for attendance and sales at the Lunt-Fontanne Theatre, and spawning several additional productions, including a National Company to tour the United States, and several foreign productions to play in many languages all over the world. After eighty-five years, *Titanic* has finally arrived in triumph in New York.

AND THE BAND PLAYED ON, TO THE VERY END.

On June 1, 1997, TITANIC received the 1997 Tony Award for Best Musical of the Broadway Season. The producers from left to right: Edward Strong, Richard S. Pechter, Robin de Levita, Michael David, Doug Johnson, Lawrence J. Wilker and Sherman Warner.

"One had to muster every shred of professionalism to face the actors with a positive attitude after each show. One night after the recalcitrant set had been particularly naughty, I went to the back of the house during the bows and leaned against the back wall of the threatre with my hands over my face. When the lights came up I realized that Michael David was standing next to me doing exactly the same thing. As our eyes met, he shook his head and said, 'Well we *are* making theatre history. . . . ' And so we did."

— LYNNE TAYLOR-CORBETT, CHOREOGRAPHER

TITANIC ATTIRE AND MODEL SHIPS

Design Sketches and Model Ships for the Production of TITANIC

By Scenic and Costume Designer

STEWART LAING

Kimono costumes designed for 1st Class passengers Mrs. Cardoza, right, and Mrs. Thayer, far right. Below, open-deck attire for millionaire passengers Mr. Astor, left, and Mr. Guggenheim,

Millionairesses Mrs. Widener and Mrs. Thayer sporting the latest in life jackets, ca. 1912. Below left, a steerage couple. Below right, three 1st Class lasses in matching, multicolored sweater sets.

Two of Stewart Laing's scale-model stage sets for, top, the 1st Class dining salon, and, bottom, the four-tiered Crow's Nest, Bridge, Main Deck and Smoke Room.

Three more models. Top, the 3rd Class dining room. Middle, a tableau for the end of Act One depicting the ship hitting the iceberg (cut from final production). Bottom, a dramatic persective for the sinking main deck.

A Composition of Titanic Proportions
Maury Yeston

THE MOMENT I REALIZED the sinking of the *Titanic* was a good idea for a Broadway musical was also, sadly, a tragic one. In late 1985 Ballard discovered the wreck on the ocean floor, and then, shockingly, within three months of that thrilling discovery in the North Atlantic, we all suffered the space shuttle *Challenger* disaster in January of 1986—this time the ship flying high above that same body of water. We, as a nation, literally reexperienced the 1912 tragedy. Once again we'd had complete blind faith in the infallibility of technology and once again, due to a small detail—in this case a faulty O-ring, not a missing pair of binoculars in the crow's nest—a dreadful loss of human life resulted. We were so overconfident that, in fact, we sent up a teacher, a non-technician, a non-astronaut. We believed our most advanced machine was so fail-safe that we could send up innocent passengers. How ironic that, once again, just as with the *Titanic*, our scientific arrogance came to a disastrous end.

Maury Yeston
*(music and
lyrics)
at rehearsal.*

I never wrestled, however, as critics later did, with the thought that the sinking of the *Titanic* wasn't "suitable" for a Broadway musical. I felt completely confident all along. I'm of

> I never wrestled with the thought that the sinking of the *Titanic* wasn't "suitable" for a Broadway musical.

the opinion that things that sound initially like "bad" ideas really can turn into great musicals, whereas things that sound like "good" ideas often don't do well. There are perfect movies that should never be turned into musicals because they are perfect the way they are, but then there are other stories that when you initially think perhaps this might not be a great idea, you begin to realize that it's precisely the element of music that gives you permission to open up a story, to delve into the inner lives of people on stage and to allow the music and the lyrics to portray their internal monologue, their internal conflicts.

And All That Jazz

It was not only the *Titanic* story which endlessly fascinates, which achieves a kind of mythic overtone, but the whole possibility of how you could portray this story musically that appealed to me. I'm schooled in that era of music. I went to college at Cambridge in England after I graduated from Yale and am familiar with the history of English symphonic repertory. It occurred to me from the start that in portraying the world of the *Titanic* I'd be portraying a world that no longer exists.

After all, the world of the Edwardians, the world of the great millionaires, the great robber barons—what Mark Twain called the Gilded Age—went down when that ship went down. And in order to create the music of that world, you have to go to the English symphonists, you have to go to Gilbert and Sullivan, and you have to go to the grand musical rhetoric of that time. It occurred to me it would be very exciting to bring that kind of dramatic musical symphonic sweep into a Broadway theatre—that it had rarely, if ever, been done before.

So, I was quite familiar with the music of the era and quite in love with it, not only from the point of view of what might be called the music of the British Empire but of the new jazz and the new ragtime that had just been created. This show was created before the show *Ragtime* and I was keenly aware of the history of American music in writing *Titanic*—the fact that "Alexander's Ragtime Band" was the hit song of 1912, along with "The Navaho Rag,"

> It was not only the *Titanic* story which endlessly fascinated . . . but the whole possibility of how you would portray this story musically that appealed to me.

John Cunningham (Captain E. J. Smith) in rehearsal.

and that the world had fallen in love with the syncopations of the new music.

I knew there was going to be ragtime in the show, just as I knew that the ragtime was going to be in precisely the place where the folks were having the (final) time of their lives because, after all, up until they hit the iceberg, everybody was having a wonderful voyage.

Very often, composer-lyricists such as myself are asked which comes first, the music or the lyrics. It's a sort of small club of people who write for the musical theatre who write both. Cole Porter in jest once answered the question by saying it was the check that came first. But the truth certainly is, for me, it's neither the music nor the lyrics that come first—it's the premise of the song, and I think that's what's not clearly understood by a lot of people who want to know about writing for the musical theatre. It's not simply a question of what are the words that they'll be singing, or what is the nature of the music, but rather "How do I musicalize this drama?" And "Why is it that somebody would sing at one point and not another?" And, in the case of the *Titanic*, the musicalization of the drama grew out of the creation of character. In the case of the opening, it grew out of the need for everyone to be aboard that ship, that they sing, "I must get on that ship" because each has a separate, private reason.

Beyond the opening, there were other moments that cried out for music: certainly the moment in the second act when I knew that the men were finally going to be separated from the women and from the children on the lifeboat deck. I knew then and there that, like many other places in musical theatre, it's the job of the composer-lyricist to find the positive inside the negative, to find hope even in the face of disaster. And so, after a long and rather arduous analysis, I wondered how is it going to be possible to portray in music and lyrics this terrible moment when the women are peeling away from the men and being put into the boats? It is almost unspeakable. And then I realized that when you have something very difficult to explain, sometimes the best way to speak of it is to describe it as you would to a child. And that was when I got the idea that we'd have a child onstage, and that the child's mother would lean down, tying a life jacket on him, and simply explain, "You and I are getting in the lifeboat, father will be staying here a while, it will be like rowing in the Serpentine. Come along now, let us have a smile." (The Serpentine is a sort-of lake in London's Hyde Park.) And from that point on we see the child torn between his mother and father. Finally, the father urges the child to go, and when they part for the last time they do something that is so fundamentally human and moving: They deny, and knowing they're never going to see each other again they nevertheless sing to each other, hoping against hope, "We'll meet tomorrow."

> It's the job of the composer-lyricist to find the positive inside the negative, to find hope even in the face of disaster.

That scene involves an element in musical theatre (Alan Jay Lerner called it "unrequited yearning") that I believe moves audiences the most; it certainly is something that moves me the most. And so we see people trapped in a situation and yet hoping against hope that somehow they'll get out of it, and that can be a very beautiful thing. But in the case of the Strauses it's totally different; they both *know* they're doomed. So what else could Mr. Straus do but look at his wife and sing to her that he loves her now just as much as he loved her on the day they were married?

The scene between the radio operator and the stoker was an idea that bubbled up in a short conversation between me and Peter Stone: "What if the stoker was afraid that his girlfriend wouldn't wait for him?" And then it occurred to us that he could dictate a marriage proposal to his girlfriend through the wireless operator on the newly invented Marconi machine. From there came a duet which really is the stoker's love song to his girlfriend and the radio operator's love song to the technology of the Marconi wireless that had just been invented.

It's absolutely necessary that the tone of the lyrics and the rhetoric of the lyrics match exactly the tone and the rhetoric of the dialogue. In some cases, actual dialogue written by Peter was musicalized, in some cases verbatim, and in some cases transformed into rhymes. There were even a few cases where a lyric got *de*musicalized and ended up being spoken. But I think the most important thing about the matching of the lyrics and the dialogue is the common

*Becky Ann Baker (Charlotte Cardoza)
during a costume fitting.*

understanding that there must be an easy flow between the spoken and sung word, a meshing of the moment where we stop speaking and we start singing. I think both Peter and I understood this very well.

On Broadway

The *Titanic* score is solidly in the Broadway tradition. It's a musical theatre piece in which the songs grow out of character and situation, in which the songs push the story forward and develop the character. We never stop simply to do a number. Everything in *Titanic* is very much along the lines of advancing the action, enhancing or increasing the suspense, or informing the audience of a conflict. There are many ways of achieving that objective. The first Broadway show I presented, *Nine*, was a series of set musical pieces, many of them star turns constructed to be show-stopping numbers. But *Titanic* was different.

Because of that, I knew the show was going to be extremely choral in nature. And that meant large groups of people all singing the same words at the same time, because the subtext simply is that they share the same thoughts and the same attitude and the same culture. Therefore it was going to be a very different show from both *Grand Hotel* and *Nine*, with their individual songs performed by individual stars. Further, *Titanic* was going to be a series of interlocking themes and motifs that were going to develop somewhat operatically. I thought that the subject matter required that kind of treatment. And I knew it was going to be very exciting once that gesture of music became orchestrated. I asked Jonathan Tunick, the show's orchestrator, if he thought we could get a sense of symphonic dimensions out of the 24 to 26 musicians in the orchestra. He assured me he could.

There are a number of multiple voice songs in the show, otherwise known as counter-melody. It is my usual style, though I think I used a great deal more of it in *Titanic* than in past shows. The whole grand sweep of the drama is the simultaneous portrayal of two and sometimes three different social classes, and what better way to do that than to have two and sometimes three different melodies and melodic elements sung simultaneously and played off against each other?

> Everything in *Titanic* is very much along the lines of advancing the action, enhancing or increasing the suspense, or informing the audience of a conflict.

Titanic Spectacle

We always knew *Titanic* would be an expensive production. There was no question in my mind that this was an opportunity to do a show in which the design element and rather spectacular stage effects would be part of both the entertainment and story-telling value of the show. Having said that, the entire book and score of *Titanic* was first performed by me and Peter, alone, with him simply reading and me sitting at the piano singing all the parts, and it worked dramatically. Successful musicals must really work as radio plays, without a stitch of costuming and without any lights or sets. Then the *addition* of the scenic elements serves to enhance. But all of the stage machinery in Hollywood wouldn't be enough to save work that's poorly constructed.

Making *Titanic* Sing

Sound designer Steve Kennedy is a man with an extraordinary talent. I was stunned by the fact that he came to early rehearsals and did all of his homework, and completely plotted out and pre-programmed the show on his sound board so that from the very first preview he was able to go from scene to scene and call up exactly the microphones he needed for each individual moment. His wonderful preparation paid off in the quality of sound he ultimately achieved. His engineering was absolutely invisible, yet it made every lyric and line of dialogue absolutely intelligible. It also created a wonderful sense of naturalism in the theatre.

Orchestrator Johathan Tunick and I have always had an extremely happy collaboration; I've done nearly all my shows with him. Furthermore, we're good friends, and see the world of music the same way. I think we both have a classical bent, we're both very literate musicians and we both enjoy reading scores. There's a very clear meeting of the minds in which he instantly understands what my musical gestures are and he possesses the uncanny knack of transforming a very highly detailed piano arrangement into an orchestral arrangement, preserving its character and its integrity, and at the same time completely transforming it.

Music supervisor—actually, conductor—Kevin Stites is a very gifted man who came to the Broadway theatre after having dominated Chicago's musical theatre. I cannot say enough good things about Kevin Stites. His talents for working with the chorus, for conducting the orchestra, and for investing energy and passion into live performance, which is really what you want from a Broadway musical director, are becoming the stuff of legend. John Miller, the music coordinator, was absolutely professional.

Judith Blazer (Caroline Neville) in rehearsal

He provided us with some of the best and most virtuosic musicians that one could ask for in a Broadway pit orchestra, not the least among them, I would point out, being John Moses on clarinet and Les Scott on flute.

Where I'm Coming From, Musically

Writing for Broadway differs absolutely from other musical forms; it's the second greatest art form created by American culture after Jazz.

Jazz and Musical Theatre are the two great interminglings of black American musical styles, European musical styles, both folk and popular, folk musical styles, elements of minstrelsy, all put together to create an entertainment that is at the same time a kind of mongrelization of all those forms and something brand new and quite wonderful. With the Musical Theatre you are always writing in the service of the drama, and always moving the story forward.

It seems to have been my predilection, as both a composer and a teacher of music, to straddle all of these worlds. In many ways, when I was a professor at Yale, I was the academic with one foot in show business, and when I was working in New York City I was the show-business writer with one foot in the academy. Because of that my music has always had influences from all these various and sundry elements.

As for the American musical specifically, I believe I received my calling at a very early age, and from two separate but equally powerful role models. I think from the moment I saw *My Fair Lady* I wanted to do *that*. And that was at age ten. But for the other great inspiration you have to go even further back into my roots, back to my seeing my mother's father who was, from time to time, a cantor in the local synagogue. When you're a very young person, and you're sitting in a great group of adults, and there's one person in the front who is singing passionately at the top of his lungs, you come to feel that that's a normal thing, or a natural thing. I don't think it's an accident that many composers for the musical theatre have had cantors in their backgrounds, either as fathers or grandfathers. Kurt Weill, George Gershwin, and Irving Berlin, to name three of the greatest. Religious singing is, I think, yet another form of musical expression feeding into the great river of the American musical theatre.

All of which is, in a way, the *Titanic* story—the positive part, where all of those different classes, and different ethnic peoples, all with a dream of doing something new, something great in the new land of America, go onto the same great ship together. I think we're all still on it, hoping for the best.

The Titanic *mates sing out.*

ACT
ONE

ACT ONE

PROLOGUE

HARLAND & WOLFF; Shipbuilders.

April 9, 1912. Entering, right, in front of the show curtain depicting an architect's rendering of *Titanic*, and crossing left, is Thomas Andrews, late 30's, shipbuilder and designer, who carries a set of rolled-up nautical blueprints.

ANDREWS
In ev'ry age mankind attempts
To fabricate great works
At once magnificent
And impossible . . .

On desert sands, from mountains of stone
A pyramid!
From flying buttresses alone
A wall of light!
A chapel ceiling
Screaming one man's ecstasy!
One man's ecstasy . . .

Miracles them all!
China's endless wall . . .

Stonehenge, the Parthenon, the Duomo . . .
The aqueducts of Rome

We did not attempt to make
With mammoth blocks of stone
A giant pyramid
No, not a pyramid . . .
Nor gothic walls that radiate with light . . .

Our task was to dream upon
And then create . . .

(Having arrived, left, he retrieves a scale model of the ship and studies it)

A floating city!
Floating city!

A human metropolis . . .
A complete civilization!
Sleek!
And fast!
At once a poem
And the perfection
Of physical engineering . . .

At once a poem
And the perfection
Of physical engineering . . .

(He continues offstage, left, as lights fade and the drop rises on:)

SCENE 1

SOUTHAMPTON. A dock, then aboard *R.M.S. Titanic*.

A gangway, marked "White Star Line," cuts diagonally across the stage, leading Off, to a great ship in the general direction of the audience.

(NOTE: The date, day, time and/or locale of the scenes and events will be shown on LED displays stage right and left.)

AT RISE: Southampton, England; Wednesday/April 10, 1912 is displayed. A young crewman—Stoker Frederick Barrett, 24—is discovered with his girlfriend. He is staring out, front, at *R.M.S. Titanic*, in wonderment.

BARRETT
How did they build Titanic?
Near a thousand feet in length
Huge beyond past endeavor
Strong beyond mortal strength

Forty-six thousand tons of steel
Eleven stories high
She's a great palace, floating
Quiet as a lullaby

(To his girl:)

Fare-thee-well, my darlin'
I'll be back before a fortnight has passed . . .

(Radioman Harold Bride, 22, and lookout Frederick Fleet, 25, have entered and now wave back to their girlfriends, offstage)

BRIDE

  Fare-thee-well, my darlin'   **FLEET & BARRETT**
  I'll be back before a fortnight has
  Passed . . .   *Fare-thee-well, my darlin'*

ALL THREE

  . . . I'll be back before a fortnight has passed . . .

  (They turn and introduce themselves)

BARRETT   Barrett—stoker off the *Baltic*—

FLEET   Fleet—lookout off the *Majestic*—

BRIDE   Harold Bride—wireless operator with the
Marconi International Marine Signal Communications
Company, Limited.

BARRETT, BRIDE & FLEET

  (They look out, at the ship, overwhelmed)

  There she is!
  Tow'ring high
  Broad and grand

Ship of dreams!

  (Add three crewmen)

Sailing day!
Morning bright
Take your flight
Ship of dreams! . . .

CREWMEN

She strains at her lines
The smoke from her funnels trailing . . .
Her prow like a knife
She'll cut through the waves unfailing . . .

Soon to be
Underway
Size and speed unexplored
And I'll be aboard
That ship of dreams!

(The light has increased; the pier is becoming increasingly busy. Capt. Edward J. Smith, a grey-bearded officer who, though speaking with a quiet voice, radiates authority and confidence, has entered and now greets the other officers as they board the ship: 1st Officer William Murdoch, 39, a Scotsman; 2nd Officer Charles Lightoller, 38; 3rd Officer Herbert Pitman, 32; 4th Officer & Navigator Joseph Boxhall, 28; and Quartermaster Robert Hitchens, 23, a Cornishman; and others; only Pitman remains on the pier, standing aside with a stevedore to oversee the loading of the ship's cargo)

STEVEDORE
7,000 heads of fresh lettuce, Titanic !

PITMAN
Morning, Mr. Lightoller

LIGHTOLLER
Morning, Mr. Pitman

PITMAN
Morning, Mr. Boxhall
Morning, Captain Smith . . .

LIGHTOLLER
Morning, Captain!

BOXHALL
Morning, Captain!

STEVEDORE
36,000 oranges, Titanic !

PITMAN
Morning, Mr. Hitchens

HITCHENS
Morning, Mr. Pitman

PITMAN
Morning, Mr. Murdoch

HITCHENS
Morning, Captain Smith

CAPT. SMITH
Morning, Murdoch . . .

MURDOCH
Morning, Captain!

CAPT. SMITH
Mr. Pitman, please
Complete the loading of the freight
And prepare for the boarding of
The serving staff and crew

PITMAN
Aye, captain!

(Now members of the ship's crew—engineers, stokers, carpenters, etc.—and the service personnel, known as hotel staff—stewards, maids, chefs, etc.—enter, along with a teen-age bellboy who greets them all by name)

CREW	**BELLBOY**
There she is . . .	*Morning, Mr. Andrews*

	Hello, Mr. Ismay
Towering high!	*Morning, Mr. Etches*
	Morning, Mr. Pitman
Broad and grand !	*Morning, Mr. Whitely*
Ship of dreams!	

STEVEDORE *42,000 fresh eggs, Titanic!*

CREW	**BELLBOY**
Sailing day . . .	*Morning, Mrs. Crawford*
	Hello, Mrs. Hutchinson
Morning bright	*Morning, Mrs. Robinson*
	Hello, Mrs. Beecham
Take your flight . . .	*Morning, Mr. Weikman!*
Ship of dreams!	

PITMAN *122,000 pounds of meat, poultry and fish, Titanic!*

STEVEDORE *40 tons of potatoes, 1,100 pounds of marmalade, 37,000 bottles of wine, beer and spirits, Titanic!*

PITMAN *55,000 china dishes and 20,000 crystal drinking glasses, Titanic!*

STEVEDORE *One Renault town carriage motorcar, Titanic!*

CREW	**BELLBOY**
Soon to be . . .	*Morning, Mr. Widgery*
	hello, Mr. Oliver
Underway . . .	*Morning, Mr. Hartley*
	Hello, Mr. Joughin
Size and speed . . .	*Cheers! Mr. Weikman*
Unexplored . . .	

ALL
. . . And I'll be aboard that ship of dreams!

(J. Bruce Ismay, late 40's, Chairman of the White Star Line, fastidiously dressed, with dark hair and a full mustache, enters along with the designer and builder, Thomas Andrews; they join Capt. Smith.)

ISMAY
Captain Smith, has there ever been
A finer morning to sail?

CAPT. SMITH
Never quite like this, Mr. Ismay
Never quite like this one, sir!

ISMAY
Mr. Andrews, has the line ever had
A faster ship for the mail?

ANDREWS
Not as fast as this, Mr. Ismay
Never quite like this one, sir!

ISMAY	**CAPT. SMITH & ANDREWS**
The pride	*The pride*

ALL THREE
Of mankind . . .
Dominion over the sea!

ISMAY

The dream

CAPT. SMITH & ANDREWS

The dream

ALL THREE

Of progress . . .
It brings great honor to me

CAPT. SMITH

To be the master . . .

ANDREWS

And the builder . . .

ISMAY

And the owner . . .

ALL THREE

Of the largest moving object in the world!

CAPT. SMITH   Mr. Pitman, begin boarding the passengers.

PITMAN

(Using a megaphone)

3rd class passengers
Proceed at once to the gangway!
Please bring your boarding documents
And await further instructions! . . .

(The 3rd-class passengers enter, emigrants from Europe and the Middle East, carrying cardboard suitcases. Among them: young Irish girls, the three Kates—McGowan, Murphey & Mullins—and Jim Farrell, a handsome Irishman. When they see the ship, Kate Mullins screams in wonder.)

KATE MURPHEY   Holy mother of god! Is that a ship or a mountain?

KATE McGOWAN   It looks long enough so a body could *walk* to America! I'm Katherine McGowan, but everyone calls me Kate.

KATE MULLINS   I'm Kate, too. Kate Mullins.

KATE MURPHEY   And I'm Kate three! Kate Murphey—

(They squeal and hug one another)

KATE MULLINS   It must be fate, then!

KATE McGOWAN   It's not fate. It's Irish.

KATE MULLINS   Are you travellin' alone?

KATE McGOWAN   Not me. I've got a feller. See that good-lookin' one up ahead?

(She indicates Jim Farrell)

I'm plannin' to marry him.

KATE MURPHEY   When's that gonna be?

KATE McGOWAN   Soon as I meet him.
Get me aboard

THREE KATES
> *Call out my name*

3RD CLASS PASSENGERS
> *It's to America we aim*
> *To find a better life*
> *We prayed to make this trip!*
> *Let all our children's children know*
> *That this day long ago*
> *We dreamt of them*
> *And came aboard this ship!*
> *For the maiden voyage!*
> *For the maiden voyage!*
> *Get us all aboard!*

PITMAN
> *Second class passengers*
> *Proceed to "C", "D" and "E" decks!*
> *Please contact the ship's purser*
> *To arrange dining assignments! . . .*

> (2nd-class passengers—professionals, shop-keepers, etc., And including Edgar & Alice Beane, middle-aged Americans with middle-west accents, and Charles Clarke with Caroline Neville, young, British, he's middle-class, she's an aristocrat—now enter and stare out at the ship in wonder)

CHARLES CLARKE
> *No account in the national press*
> *Has quite done justice to this!*

EDGAR BEANE
> *It's a sight for once in a lifetime!*

BEANES, CHARLES & CAROLINE
> *Yes, a sight for once in a lifetime!*

CHARLES CLARKE
> *And the chance to run away*
> *And marry now*
> *We two daren't miss!*

CAROLINE NEVILLE
> *It's a chance for once in a lifetime!*

2ND CLASS PASSENGERS
> *Yes, a chance for once in a lifetime!*
>
> *Can't wait to board that ship today*
> *Be with her when she pulls away*
> *And takes her maiden sail*
> *I must get on that ship*
> *The largest, grandest on the earth*
> *And I've reserved a berth*
> *To be aboard, now point me toward*
> *That ship!*

ALICE BEANE
> *The finest people will attend*
> *The best among them we'll befriend*
> *They'll stand right next to us*
> *Be at my fingertip . . .*

ALL
> *Great heads of state and millionaires*
> *Who run the world's affairs*

> *Will all be there*
> *I must get on that ship!*
> *For the maiden voyage!*
> *For the maiden voyage!*
> *Get us all aboard!*

PITMAN   1st Class passengers occupying the deluxe suites on "A" and "B" Decks are requested to board at this time!—

> (Alice Beane follows Pitman as he goes to greet the 1st-class passengers)

EDGAR BEANE   Come back, Alice—

ALICE BEANE   I want to see them, Edgar—

> (The 1st-class passengers enter. First come John Jacob Astor, 47, and his noticeably pregnant wife, Madeleine, 19. Henry Etches, 50, Senior 1st Class Steward, joins Pitman)

PITMAN
> *Colonel John Jacob Astor*
> *And Mrs. Astor, too!*
> *Arriving now from the boat train*
> *Direct from Waterloo Station*
> *May proceed to their parlour suite*
> *A-62!*

ALICE BEANE
> *Her name is Madeleine*
> *She's John Jacob Astor's second wife*
> *She's only nineteen-years-old*
> *And now she's married to a prominent man*
> *Worth over a hundred and fifty million*
> *And twenty-nine years her senior*

lionaire, accompanied by Mme. Aubert, an attractive French woman, enters)

PITMAN   —Mr. Benjamin Guggenheim and party will find his customary suite on "A" deck!—

ALICE BEANE
  Made his money by smelting gold
  Spends it like water
  Forty-five hundred dollars for
  The Louis Quatorze suite!
  So he can live in luxurious sin
  With his latest mistress
  And they call that justice?
  They call that justice? . . .

    (George & Eleanor Widener enter)

PITMAN   —Mr. and Mrs. George Widener may proceed to promenade suite B-51!—

ALICE BEANE
  He's the richest man in Philadelphia! . . .

    (John & Marion Thayer enter with a nine-year-old boy)

PITMAN   —Mr. and Mrs. John B. Thayer and family, Promenade Suite B-58!—

ALICE BEANE
  Vice-president of the Pennsylvania Railroad! . . .

    (Mrs. Cardoza, a handsome woman in her 40s, enters)

They've only been married seven months
she's already seven months pregnant
and the scandal was such
they ran away to Europe to avoid the publicity
avoid the publicity . . .

    (The Strauses—Isidor & Ida, both in their late 60s—are next to enter)

PITMAN   Mr. and Mrs. Isidor Straus may proceed to Parlour Suite B-55!—

ALICE BEANE
  Aren't they modest?
  You'd never think by looking at them
  That he and his brother own Macy's Department Store
  Own Macy's Department Store
  Outright!
  And he was close advisor
  To President Grover Cleveland
  And served in the House of Representatives
  Two full terms!
  And that's his wife of forty years, named Ida
  Sad! She hasn't been well
  So the two of them have been wintering
  On the French Riviera
  French Riviera . . .

    (Benj. Guggenheim, the very model of an American mil-

PITMAN   —Mrs. Charlotte Drake Cardoza, Suite B-54!—

ALICE BEANE
No one really knows who she is
But the newspaper says she booked
The most expensive suite on the ship
And travels with fourteen steamer trunks
A medicine chest
Her personal pillows and sheets
And four little Pekinese dogs
So she must be somebody
She must be somebody . . .

PITMAN
    (Blows a whistle)

Last call for boarding!
This is the very last call for boarding!

ALL
    (as they go up gangway)

Lift up the ramp
Let go the lines
Raise up her colours and designs
Prepare for casting off
And through the port we'll slip
each person standing at the rail
Let one great thought prevail
One single prayer:
God bless this noble ship!

PITMAN
    ALL ASHORE WHO ARE GOING ASHORE!
    ALL ASHORE WHO ARE GOING ASHORE!

PITMAN   I report this ship loaded and ready for sea!

CAPT. SMITH   Lower the gangways, Mr. Pitman!

PITMAN   Gangways lowered, captain!

CAPT. SMITH   Make fast the tugs!

PITMAN   Tugs all fast, sir!

CAPT. SMITH   Let go all lines!

PITMAN   Let go the stern lines!—Let go the bow lines!—Let go aft springs!—

CAPT. SMITH   Tow her off, Mr. Pitman!

    (The scene changes to: Aboard *R.M.S. Titanic*:
    the poop deck at the stern of the ship)

FULL COMPANY
    Farewell, farewell
    Godspeed, Titanic!
    From your berth glide free
    As you plough the deep
    In your arms I'll keep

Wait! Come back! You've got to come back! I told everyone I was crossing on the *Titanic*! What am I going to tell them now?! I'll be the laughing stock of Poughkeepsie!—

(He realizes it's hopeless)

I don't believe it.

(He drops his suitcases)

If that isn't the story of my entire goddam life—

(The scene changes to:)

SCENE 2

THE BRIDGE. And later, BOILER ROOM #6.

ABOVE: THE BRIDGE, on the boat deck, contains a large helm, brass binnacle, telephone, ship's telegraph, map table and a message board.

AT RISE: "Ship's Bridge; Thursday/April 11" is displayed. Present are: Capt. Smith, Officers Murdoch, Lightoller, and, at the helm, Quartermaster Hitchens. Four bells sound.

MURDOCH
We've cleared Wolf Rock, sir

CAPT. SMITH Thank you, Mr. Murdoch. What's our present course?

LIGHTOLLER
West by north, 2-8-1 degrees, sir.

Safely west
May you carry me . . .

(During this the young boy will weave among them, playing with a toy model boat)

Sail on, sail on
Great ship Titanic!
Cross the open sea
Pray the journey's sound
Till your port be found
Fortune's winds
Sing godspeed to thee . . .
Fortune's winds
Sing godspeed
To thee!

(As the scene starts to change: Downstage, back on the pier: an American, Frank Carlson, enters on the run, a large valise in each hand)

CARLSON   Gangway!—gangway, everybody!—my car broke down!—hold the ship—!

(He stops when he sees that the ship has sailed without him)

CAPT. SMITH
    Steady as she goes, Quartermaster.

HITCHENS
    Aye, aye, Captain

CAPT. SMITH   Mr. Lightoller, what's our present speed?

LIGHTOLLER
    Nineteen knots, sir

CAPT. SMITH   Maintain 19 knots, Mr. Murdoch.

MURDOCH
    Aye, aye, sir

      (He goes to the telephone)

Boiler rooms 1 through 6—maintain 68 revolutions of the wing propellers.

      (Ismay barges in, followed by Henry Etches, 50, Senior 1st Class Steward, who carries a bottle of champagne and glasses)

ISMAY   E. J.! Now that we're officially underway, I thought a little celebration might be in order.

CAPT. SMITH   I'm sorry, Mr. Ismay, I don't allow alcohol on my bridge. You know that, Mr. Etches.

ETCHES   Yes, sir, I do.

ISMAY (A tight smile)   Technically speaking, E. J., it could be considered my bridge.

CAPT. SMITH   Not at sea, Mr. Ismay.

ETCHES (He's quietly opened the bottle and examined it) I'm terrible sorry, sir—I'm afraid this bottle seems to have gone completely flat. I couldn't possibly allow you to drink it. Would you like me to fetch another, Mr. Ismay?

ISMAY   Oh, never mind, let it go.

ETCHES   Thank you, sir. Again, my apologies.

CAPT. SMITH   Thank you, Mr. Etches.

      (Etches goes)

ISMAY   Yes, well—with or without champagne, I want to toast our ship: the *Royal Mail Steamer Titanic*—nearly a quarter mile in length, she's bigger, grander and safer than any ship in history, the greatest achievement in transatlantic naviga-

tion since that very first crossing 420 years ago.

>   (Andrews enters, with his set of plans in hand, as always)

Ah, Andrews, I'm glad you're here. I was just congratulating the three of us on our magnificent contribution to the 20th century.

>   (Again raising his empty glass)

Progress, gentlemen! I give you progress.

CAPT. SMITH   I trust you'll excuse us, Mr. Ismay. We have our duties—

ISMAY   Tell me, E. J.—what's our present speed?

CAPT. SMITH   19 knots, Mr. Ismay.

ISMAY   Really. I would have expected us to be going faster now that we've cleared land. I want us to make New York by Tuesday afternoon. Tell me, Andrews—I understand that 22 knots would be necessary in order to make a six-day crossing. In your expert opinion is *Titanic* capable of that speed?

>   (As Andrews glances at Smith)

Come, come, Andrews, you're the one who built the thing— are we capable of 22 knots?

ANDREWS   Capable. Yes, sir, I'm sure we are. Possibly a bit more if pushed—23 perhaps—but—

ISMAY   *Excellent, sir!* I'm very pleased to hear it!

ANDREWS   *But*—it is customary for a maiden voyage to proceed prudently.

ISMAY   It's the maiden voyage that creates news, dammit! And I intend for this one to create a legend! So answer me straight, man—when can we expect to run at full speed?

ANDREWS   When the captain orders it, sir.

ISMAY   Then we must persuade him to do so, mustn't we?

CAPT. SMITH (A beat)   In point of fact, Mr. Ismay, I was about to give the order when you walked in. Mr. Murdoch— increase speed to 20 knots.

MURDOCH   20 knots, aye, aye, sir.

>   (Picks up the telephone)

Increase steam, Mr. Bell—give us 71 revolutions.

ISMAY   20 knots. Well, it's a start, I suppose. Carry on, gentlemen—

>   (Turns and goes)

CAPT. SMITH   Watch your compass, Mr. Hitchens—you're drifting off course.

HITCHENS   I don't think so, sir—

CAPT. SMITH   Don't argue with me, man! If I say you're off course then you're bloody well off course!

>   (BELOW: lights up on boiler room #6 on the Orlop [lowest] deck: there are 3 boilers, rear, with coal furnaces. Three stokers, including Frederick Barrett, shovel the coal into the furnaces. The Chief Engineer, Joseph Bell, is in charge. "Boiler room #6" is displayed)

BELL   Set your screws to 71, Mr. Barrett—!

BARRETT   71? If you ask me, Mr. Bell, it's a mite soon for 71—

BELL   Captain's orders, Mr. Barrett! If you've got no objections, that is—

BARRETT (Shrugging, he adjusts some gauges)   It's his ship, isn't it? 71 it shall be. But I'll speak plain, Mr. Bell—if it was my ship, I wouldn't recommend her speed increased too quick.

BELL   Do as you're told, Mr. Barrett.

BARRETT
> *She's sparkling clean, this new-born ship*
> *But one old thing is clear*
> *The orders they propose above*
> *We execute down here . . . .*
> *We'll watch from here as up above*
> *They'll catch a whiff of glory*
> *This wonder ship may be brand new*

But it's the same old story . . .

(As the stokers go to work shoveling coal:)

Stoke the fire in the hold
As the men draw back . . .
Feed the heat in the hold
As the men draw back
And the dust of the coal in the air is black
And a trickle of sweat runs down your back . . .

And what are the boys from the Midlands doing here?

Coal it is that makes the steam
That runs the machines that run the world
That sends the men below the ground
To mine the coal
Each day . . .

From Leicestershire and Nottingham
Us lads who worked down in the pit
Knew if you got above the ground
You'd save your soul
Some way . . .

Get out of the pit
And westward I knew I could run
And ship out to sea and there my new life was begun .
. .

And the screws were turning at seventy-one . . .
It became my dream to go out to sea . . .
Further out from the mine
You couldn't be . . .

(ON THE BRIDGE: Capt. Smith is showing a passenger, Mme. Aubert, around)

But, born to the coal, there's no place for you else-
where
You trade a life of dank and gloom
To shovel in the boiler room
But now you're seven decks below
A lady's dainty feet . . .

And nothing has changed
There's nothing a miner can do
The pit and your mates
Turned into the hold and the crew . . .
And the screws are turning at seventy-two . . .

Faster and faster we watch as we gain evermore
Seventy-three, and too soon it is seventy-four . . .

For a record speed I believe we strive!
For the maiden trip that's too hard to drive
If you push her faster than seventy-five.

That is the truth
I swear!

(BLACKOUT. The scene changes to:)

SCENE 3

THE SALOON ("D") DECK: a 2nd class promenade; then
inside the 1st class dining saloon.

ON THE DECK: a line of large portholes punctuate the
ship's superstructure.

AT RISE: "'D' deck; Thursday/April 11" is displayed. Edgar
& Alice Beane enter. She is reading a guide of the ship
as she stops to look through one of the portholes.

ALICE BEANE
Edgar, look!
Right in there!
What a sight!
The 1st class dining saloon . . .

Saloon—?

EDGAR BEANE   Come on, Alice, they want us to get the
hell to our own saloon—

ALICE BEANE   Language, Edgar. Did you get a good look
at John Jacob Astor? He looks exactly like his picture!

EDGAR BEANE   So do you, Alice.

ALICE BEANE   Oh Edgar, this is so exciting. Almost every
famous millionaire in the whole world is on this ship!
And to think we'll actually be rubbing elbows with them!

How impressed
They'll all be
When they hear
All that you know about hardware!

EDGAR BEANE   Yeah, well, I wouldn't exactly count on
"rubbing elbows" with them, Alice. They won't allow us
peasants in 2nd class to go anywhere near those people
in there.

ALICE BEANE   What's the point of being on the same
boat if we can't hobnob with them?! It's bad enough that
we have to make do with that dinky cabin they gave us
with those two silly little bunk beds—

EDGAR BEANE (Suggestively)   We don't have to use the
top one, Alice—

ALICE BEANE   Calm down, Edgar. I'm telling you right
now—I'm going in there. If it's the last thing I do I'm
going in there.

EDGAR BEANE   Dammit, alice—

ALICE BEANE   Language, Edgar—

EDGAR BEANE   —They don't want us in there. They want
us right here, where we are. That's all we paid for and
that's all we get.

ALICE BEANE (To herself)   Well, that's not all I'm getting.

(She goes. As he follows her offstage: Charles
Clarke & Caroline Neville enter. She, too, cannot resist looking through the porthole.)

CAROLINE NEVILLE
Charles, look there!
Through that glass
There's first class
For all your posh, smart people . . .

CHARLES CLARKE   Rich people, you mean—

CAROLINE NEVILLE   Of course they're rich, darling—
they're Americans. Can't you just imagine what they'll all

CHARLES CLARKE Why not? That's what we would be if your snob of a father had permitted it. And that is exactly what we *will* be the minute we arrive in America.

CAROLINE NEVILLE Darling, considering our living arrangements, everyone on board thinks we're *already* married.

CHARLES CLARKE You know perfectly well we would have separate cabins if I could have afforded them.

CAROLINE NEVILLE Yes, but separate cabins would have meant separate beds, Charles.

CHARLES CLARKE Yes, well, we had to make do with what we had, didn't we?

(They start offstage)

You don't suppose we'll burn in hell for it, do you?

CAROLINE NEVILLE Stop worrying, darling—in America it's not a sin at all.

CHARLES CLARKE What isn't?

CAROLINE NEVILLE Saving money.

(They laugh and he kisses her lightly as they go. Now 1st Class Steward Etches enters, followed by another 1st Class Steward, Andrew Latimer)

ETCHES
My dear Mr. Latimer!
Prepare to greet our clientele
Our meeting is imminent
Our having just rung the dinner bell
It won't be a novelty
We mostly have seen them all before . . .

Prepare for the usual
You should be aware of what's in store . . .
We've served them on the Baltic
And the Oceanic, Olympic and Majestic
And today's the same
There's nothing changed . . .

Mr. Astor takes his toast dry
Mrs. Straus likes the grouse
With the sauce on the side
And the Wideners love kidney pie
Bring it hot, if it's not
They'll be fit to be tied

They're accustomed to the best
Of all that money buys
The world of free enterprise
Has given this privilege to the rich . . .

When they're idle
They're entitled to the luxury
Which we provide
That's forever the source of our pride...
Which is why we're always there

be jabbering about? All those things my father lives for: international banking, venture capital, cornering the market—you know, *that* sort of thing.

CHARLES CLARKE How would I know "*that* sort of thing," Caroline? My father never had a corner on the market. All he ever had was a market on the corner. I warned you running away with me would be educational—

Caroline!
Aren't you thrilled?
Finally now
You'll see what second class looks like!

CAROLINE NEVILLE Oh, Charles, I love it when you're sarcastic. It makes me feel like we're a real married couple.

With our especial form of care
For every hungry millionaire
By now they've all arrived . . .

(The Scene Changes to: Inside the 1st-CLASS DINING SALOON: an ornate and luxurious ship's restaurant. At the center is the large "captain's table," with two smaller tables Right and Left.

"1st Class/Dining Saloon; Thursday/April 11" is displayed.

Several 1st class passengers enter: J. J. & Madeleine Astor, Benj. Guggenheim & Mme. Aubert, John & Marion Thayer, George & Eleanor Widener, Ida & Isidor Straus, Mrs. Cardoza, the Major, late 60s, a retired British officer in mufti but wearing his many medals, Ismay and others. The waiting staff distribute glasses of champagne before preparing to serve the meal)

1ST CLASS PASSENGERS
We're sailing aboard the greatest ship

That ever sailed the seas
The hull and the keel imperviously
Stronger by degrees!

THEIR WIVES
Magnificent crystal chandeliers
Parquet [par-quette] in all the floors

ALL
The ceiling is Jacobean
A decor their world adores

(Split chorus; alternating)

Remarkable ship   Oh what a ship!
Remarkable keel   Oh what a keel!
Remarkable steel   Oh what a ship!

(Together)

If it could be put in a phrase . . . It's
"What a remarkable age this is!"

MEN
A fellow's invented see-through film
He calls it "cellophane!"

ALL
Another has built a parachute
For jumping out of an airplane!
Remarkable things flow endlessly
From out the human brain!
Indeed, and what a remarkable age this is!

ETCHES   (Again addressing his staff:)
Keep the Captain's table pristine
Here we seat the elite whom we happily serve
Here they dine on fine French cuisine
It's the crème de la crème's
Exclusive preserve!

It's the pleasure of the leisure class's greatest wits
To be where the Captain sits
When taking their dinner on the sea
Giving def'rence to their pref'rences is OUR chief art!
We play a part
In a perfectly working machine

You should ever be aware
This is a privilege great and rare
A special burden that we bear
In our respective lives!

MILLIONAIRES
Remarkable U. S. Steel
Is splitting shares at five to four!
Monopoly makes the industry
Far better than before!

MILLIONAIRE'S WIVES
Attending the coronation of
King George the Fifth was grand

ETCHES
And afterwards off to Monaco
To frolic in the sand

(Split chorus; alternating)

Remarkable talk   Oh what a talk!
Remarkable times   Oh what a time!
Remarkable world   Oh what a world!

(Together)

So much to surprise and amaze . . .
And . . .

MILLIONAIRES & WIVES	ETCHES & STAFF
What a remarkable time	
What a remarkable world	
What a remarkable age . . .	*The hull and the keel*
	impervious
	magnificent crystal
	chandeliers
	a fellow's invented
	see-through film
	and what a remarkable
	age . . .

ALL
This . . . is!

(As Capt. Smith arrives: they all sit, Smith at one end of the large table, the Astors, Thayers, Wideners, Guggenheim and Mme. Aubert fill in, with Ismay at the opposite end, facing Smith, and the Major dead center. The other 1st class passengers—among them, Mr. & Mrs. Straus and Mrs. Cardoza—have gone to smaller tables, right and left.

In the back, a three-piece string ensemble led by Bandmaster Wallace Hartley, all wearing black jackets, has begun playing "Palm Court" music)

BELLBOY   The dinner seating for Thursday, April 11th, is now being served in the First Class Dining Saloon!

THE MAJOR   Never forget my last tour in India during the Tirah campaign of '97 to reopen the Khyber Pass when we were ambushed by 8,000 crazed, godless savages who attacked without—

ISMAY (interrupting)   E. J.! Have you ever had so many distinguished Americans in your charge at one time? You know most of them, I'm sure. And, of course, everyone knows the Major—

CAPT. SMITH   Of course. Welcome aboard. Mr. Guggenheim, you're becoming quite a regular on the Atlantic run.

BENJ. GUGGENHEIM   Yes, in point of fact this is my 34th crossing.

ISMAY   E. J.! You haven't told us how many miles we covered yesterday.

CAPT. SMITH   484, Mr. Ismay.

ISMAY   Are you pleased with that?

CAPT. SMITH   Yes, I am, sir. It's better than I expected for the first day.

ISMAY   In that case I'm sure we'll do even better today.

(1st Officer Murdoch has entered and now approaches Capt. Smith; the music stops)

MURDOCH   Begging your pardon, Captain—Mr. Hitchens has requested his course.

CAPT. SMITH   Increase speed, Mr. Murdoch, to 21 knots and tell Mr. Hitchens to set course at west, northwest, 2-9-2 degrees.

MURDOCH   That's the northern track, sir.

CAPT. SMITH   I'm well aware of that, Mr. Murdoch.

(With a glance at Ismay)

It will save us both coal and time. At least three hours.

ISMAY   Three hours! Oh, well done, E. J.!

(As Murdoch goes, the bellboy again enters with his triangle.)

BELLBOY   The dinner seating for Friday, April 12th, is now being served in the First Class Dining Saloon!

(It's now the next day. "Friday/April 12" is displayed. Hartley and his ensemble resume playing)

THE MAJOR   Don't believe I told you about my forced march to the Sudan during the winter of '85 to relieve the attack on "Chinese" Gordon by the Mahdi and 6,000 of his crazed, godless savages who came down with their spears—

ISMAY (Interrupting)   E. J.! We're all quite anxious to know *yesterday's* mileage.

CAPT. SMITH   519, Mr. Ismay.

ISMAY   Much better!

(Radioman Harold Bride has entered and now approaches Capt. Smith; the music stops)

BRIDE   I'm—I'm sorry to disturb your meal, captain—

CAPT. SMITH   Who the devil are you?

BRIDE   Second Wireless Operator Bride, sir. With the Marconi International Marine Radio-telegraphy and Signal Communications Company, Limited?

CAPT. SMITH   What is it, Mr. Bride?

BRIDE   Message, sir—from the Furness Liner *Rappahannock* four days out of Halifax. She reports an iceberg—

CAPT. SMITH (Quickly, taking the paper from him) Thank you, Mr. Bride, I can read.

BRIDE   Right. I mean, aye, aye—sir—

(Awkwardly, he goes. The bellboy enters yet again, striking his triangle)

BELLBOY   The dinner seating for Saturday, April 13th, is now being served in the First Class Dining Saloon!

(It's the next day. "Saturday/April 13" is displayed. Hartley and his ensemble resume playing)

THE MAJOR —But the proudest moment of my entire career came in aught-two under the command of Kitchener at Johannesburg when untold thousands of crazed, godless savages appeared without warning—

ELEANOR WIDENER (Interrupting) Mrs. Astor—I understand this was your first trip to Europe—

J. J. ASTOR But not her last, Mrs. Widener—certainly not her last—

MARION THAYER And how did you find Paris, Mrs. Astor?

MADELEINE ASTOR Thank goodness I didn't have to. Jake knew right where it was.

(2nd Officer Lightoller has entered and now approaches Capt. Smith; the music stops)

LIGHTOLLER Excuse me, captain—

CAPT. SMITH Yes, Mr. Lightoller?

LIGHTOLLER Have you any instructions, sir, concerning our present speed?

CAPT. SMITH Maintain 21 knots, Mr. Lightoller.

LIGHTOLLER 21 knots. Yes, sir.

(He goes)

ISMAY 21 knots? Come, come, E. J.—I've promised these gentlemen we'll arrive in New York before nightfall Tuesday. At this rate we'll never make it!

CAPT. SMITH (Annoyed) I'm afraid it's too soon for *either* of us to say, Mr. Ismay.

(He rises from the table)

I trust you'll forgive me. Please continue with your meal.

MARION THAYER Oh, must you leave us, Captain?

CAPT. SMITH Unfortunately, Mrs. Thayer, my duties on the bridge, though not nearly so pleasant as sitting here with you attractive ladies, require my attention. Please excuse me.

(He goes)

MAJOR
Remarkable man our Capt. Smith!

MAJOR & MILLIONAIRES
Remarkable man our Capt. Smith!

PASSENGERS
Remarkable man our
  Capt. Smith!
Remarkable man our
  Capt. Smith!   ETCHES & STAFF
Remarkable man our   *Remarkable man*
  Capt. Smith!
Remarkable!   *Remarkable*
Remark . . .   *. . . Markable*
Remarkable   *Markable man!*

Talk   *Oh what a talk!*
Remarkable times   *Oh what a time!*

Remarkable world   *Oh what a world*
    (together)
So much to surprise and amaze . . .
And . . .

MILLIONAIRES & WIVES
What a remarkable time
What a remarkable world
What a remarkable age . . .
This . . .
Is!

BELLBOY Sweets and after-dinner liqueurs are now being served in the Café Parisien!

(The scene changes to:)

SCENE 4

THE BRIDGE.

Saturday afternoon, immediately after. "Ship's Bridge; Saturday/April 13" is displayed. Murdoch is in command, Lightoller at the helm. Capt. Smith enters.

CAPT. SMITH What's our position, Mr. Murdoch?

MURDOCH
Latitude forty-two, thirty-five north
Longitude forty-five, fifty west, Captain

CAPT. SMITH And the sea temperature, Mr. Lightoller?

LIGHTOLLER
Last check, down five degrees
To thirty-four Fahrenheit, sir

MURDOCH
(Handing him a message)
Another communication, Captain . . .

Ice warning from *Coronian*—

CAPT. SMITH Another one?

MURDOCH They've sighted a large berg at 41-50 north by 49-52 west.

CAPT. SMITH Plot the position with the other reports we've received.

(He returns the message)

MURDOCH It's directly on our new course, sir—

CAPT. SMITH Not to worry. At least 600 miles off.

MURDOCH Still—

CAPT. SMITH Not to worry. We'll keep a sharp eye, eh? And Mr. Murdoch—increase speed to 22 knots.

MURDOCH 22, Captain?

CAPT. SMITH Yes. Let's do everything we can to avoid bringing Mr. Ismay to the bridge again.

MURDOCH (Smiling) Yes, sir.

(Picks up the telephone)

Engine room—increase speed to 78 revolutions of the wing propellers.

CAPT. SMITH   If I remember correctly, Mr. Murdoch, you qualified for your master's papers when you were only 25—youngest man in the Line's history. But here you are, still without a ship of your own. What are you waiting for, Mr. Murdoch?

MURDOCH   The master of a ship carries a heavy responsibility, Captain.

CAPT. SMITH   Every single minute, Mr. Murdoch.

MURDOCH   I'm just not certain I'm up to it, sir.

CAPT. SMITH   A ship's master must be certain of *every-thing*, Mr. Murdoch. Even when he's not. And I'm as certain of that, as I am that this is my final crossing.

MURDOCH (Surprised)   Captain—?

CAPT. SMITH   After 43 years of service, I informed the Line of my wish to retire. But they asked me to stay on, to see them through the maiden voyage. My wife was disappointed, of course. But how could I refuse? Take over, Mr. Murdoch.

   (He goes)

MURDOCH
   Thousands on board
   Each in his class

You are the master of all that must pass
Yours to set course
Yours to command
You hold their souls
In the palm of your hand
You hold their souls
In the palm of your hand

   (The lights fade on the Bridge)

SCENE 5

THE MIDDLE ("F") DECK: THE 3RD CLASS COMMISSARY

In sharp contrast to the 1st Class Dining Saloon, here there are only plain wooden chairs and tables and no decoration of any kind.

AT RISE: "3rd Class Dining saloon; Saturday/April 13" is displayed; it is late afternoon of the same day. At the tables several 3rd-class passengers of various nationalities, and including Kate McGowan, Kate Murphey, Kate Mullins, and Jim Farrell are grouped in the same positions as were the passengers in the 1st Class Saloon.

(NOTE: the 1st class passengers seen in their Dining Saloon are now 3rd-class passengers, and arranged at tables in an identical configuration.)

3RD CLASS STEWARD   3rd class passengers are reminded not to take food below to your cabins!

KATE MULLINS (To the steward)   What's the reason for that, then?

3RD CLASS STEWARD   It encourages the rats.

KATE MURPHEY   They got rats on a brand new ship?

3RD CLASS STEWARD   They're always the first aboard.

KATE McGOWAN   Well, they're welcome to have part of my share. Sure and me entire family could live a *week* off just what I been leavin' on me plate. And all of it for free!

JIM FARRELL   *Free?* Are you daft, then? And, why do you suppose they charged us every bit of 60 shillings for our passage? What do I need with all this fine cloth and electrical light?

KATE McGOWAN   Well, Jim Farrell, I'm gonna have fine cloth, electrical light and a whole lot more when I get to America. Includin' me own personal bathtub. I'm gonna rise straight to the top, I will, just like cream!

> I will be a proper person
> People will look up to me
> What a girl that girl McGowan
> Katie Violet Maud Marie
> I aspire to heights of glory
> In the New World
> That can be!
> In that grandest nation I'll stand tall
> Reach my very highest hopes
> Of all . . .

I'm aimin' to have a real profession, I am!

KATE MULLINS   Me, too!

KATE MURPHEY   Me, three!

KATE McGOWAN
> I want to be a lady's maid!
> Lady's maid in America
> In America the streets are paved with gold

KATE MURPHEY
> I want to be a governess
> Governess in America
> In America it's better I am told

KATE MULLINS
> I want to be a sewing girl
> Sewing girl in America
> In America I'll sew till I am old . . .

KATE McGOWAN
> There's a place called Chicago
> I've seen it on the map

KATE MURPHEY
> There's a place called Mary-land
> I've seen it on the map

KATE MULLINS
> There's a place in America
> Called Albuquerque [al-ber-kyew-kyew]
> And I'm hopin' it's a bit like Donegal

KATE McGOWAN
> Oh, I'm hopin' that it is . . .

THREE KATES
> There I'm hopin' that it is . . .
> Where my dreamin' and my hopin' and my schemin'
> And my prayin' and my wishin' to be happy
> Will come true enough
> And . . .

1ST MAN (MR.THAYER)
> I want to be an engineer . . .   KATE McGOWAN
> An engineer . . .   Oh, I will be grand . . .
>
> In America   MURPHEY & McGOWAN
> The streets are paved   In America
>   with gold   the streets are paved with
>   gold

2ND MAN (MR. WIDENER)
> I want a shop to call my own   THREE KATES
> To call my own . . .   Oh, I will be grand . . .
>
> In America   MURPHEY & McGOWAN
> It's better I am told   In America
>   It's better I am told . . .

ALL
> Oh, far beyond the Northern Sea
> A new life can unfold
>
> And I'm planning that it will
> How I'm planning that it will
> Where my dreamin' and my hopin' and my schemin'
> And my prayin' and my wishin' to be happy
> Will come true enough
> and . . .

3RD MAN (MR. GUGGENHEIM)
> I want to be a millionaire!
> Millionaire in america
> Strike it rich and spend the fortune I amass . . .

4TH MAN (MAJOR)
> I want to be a constable!
> Constable in America
> In America you rise above your class . . .

ALL
> Oh, there's the place your industry and talent
> Can be sold . . .

KATE McGOWAN
> And I'm certain that it will . . .

THREE KATES
> There I'm certain that it will . . .

GERMAN MAN [ISIDOR STRAUS]
> Ich will ein gutes leben haben . . .

ITALIAN MAN & WOMAN [THE ASTORS]   ALL
> Una bella vita negli stati uniti . . .   Ah

ALL
> Where my dreamin' and my hopin' and my schemin'
> And my prayin' and my wishin' to be happy
> Will come true enough
> And . . .
> I want to rise above myself . . .
>   . . . Oh, I will be grand

TENOR & SOPRANOS
In America, the streets
Are paved with gold . . .

> **3 KATES & FARRELL**
> *In America, the streets*
> *Are paved with gold . . .*

> > **ALTOS & BASSES**
> > *In America, the streets*
> > *Are paved with gold . . .*

KATE McGOWAN
I want to be a lady's maid . . .

3RD MAN (MR. GUGGENHEIM)
Millionaire . . .

1ST MAN (MR.THAYER)
Engineer . . .

ALL
In America!

KATE McGOWAN
(By herself, to herself)

Better place for me and you . . .
Better land to start anew . . .
Better land for the baby . . .
That I
Hold

(The scene changes to:)

SCENE 6

THE BRIDGE.

AT RISE: Lightoller and Murdoch are there, the latter at the helm. Andrews is checking various instruments and taking notes. "Ship's Bridge; Saturday, April 13" is displayed.

MURDOCH   It's turning bloody cold isn't it, Mr. Lightoller—

LIGHTOLLER   Yes. It feels rather more like February than April.

(Ismay enters)

ISMAY   Ah, Andrews! There you are! I've been looking for you everywhere. I want your opinion on how you think the crossing is going so far.

ANDREWS   Not as well as I'd hoped, Mr. Ismay. We've got a few problems.

ISMAY (Concerned)   Really? Such as what?

ANDREWS   I'm disappointed in the water pressure for the upper decks. And the kitchen staff are complaining that their sleeping quarters are over-heated—

ISMAY   There's gratitude for you. In my father's day they were lucky to get any heat at all. Now tell me, Andrews—are you satisfied with our present speed?

ANDREWS   I think so, sir.

ISMAY   Well, I don't mind telling you I'm very disappointed. The sea is calm, the weather's fair—why aren't we going faster?

ANDREWS   We're doing 22 knots, Mr. Ismay. That's better than any White Star ship's ever managed.

ISMAY   Answer me straight, Andrews: You chaps at Harland and Wolff built the Cunard ship, too—was Titanic *intentionally* designed to run slower?

ANDREWS   I really must protest the implication, sir. When your father ran the line he demanded safety and comfort *before* speed. Cunard may get their passengers there a little faster, yes. But White Star gives 'em a far better ride.

ISMAY   It's a new world, Andrews. These days people want speed above everything else. Americans would gladly lose their dinner over the rail if it meant arriving in New York a day sooner.

(Capt. Smith has entered)

CAPT. SMITH   Mr. Ismay—is there something you wanted, sir?

ISMAY   E. J.! I was wondering if you could now predict with any certainty our arriving in New York by Tuesday afternoon.

CAPT. SMITH   I can only say it's still possible.

ISMAY   *Possible?!* But it's *imperative,* dammit! If we have to stand off until Wednesday morning our return to England will be delayed a full 24 hours! *Titanic must* be known as a six-day ship, E. J.—even the bloody *krauts* can do it! And if second-rate tubs like *Deutschland* and *Kaiser Wilhelm* can turn around in a fortnight, then so, by God, shall we!

(This outburst creates an awkward silence. Finally:)

CAPT. SMITH   I'm sure that we will do everything we can, Mr. Ismay.

ISMAY   Splendid. That's all one can ask, isn't it?

(As he turns and goes: The sound of a telegraphic transmission is heard, the dots and dashes of the ship's wireless; the scene changes to:)

SCENE 7

THE RADIO ROOM

A small, cluttered cabin filled with radio equipment of the era, all of it bearing the Marconi label. "Radio Room; Saturday/April 13" is displayed

AT RISE: Late Saturday night. Radioman Bride, wearing earphones, sits hunched over his key, furiously sending messages in Morse code, copying from a tall stack of forms. As he finishes one he impales it on a spike and as he begins the next, Stoker Frederick Barrett enters and removes his cap.

BARRETT 'Scuse me —

    (No answer, louder:)

BARRETT 'Scuse me—!

BRIDE (He continues working) Who's there?

BARRETT Barrett. *Barrett!*

BRIDE (Turning, taking off his earphones) The stoker, I remember! Welcome to the most important place on the whole ship. What can I do for you, Barrett?

BARRETT I heard you could actually send a message back to England.

BRIDE You heard right, all right. Sitting right here I can communicate with important people all over the world.

BARRETT Yeah?

BRIDE (Hearing a signal, he puts on his earphones) I'd explain how it works, but I'm afraid—Hold on! There's a message coming in—iceberg warning—from the *Baltic*,

that's your old ship—

BARRETT Yeah?

BRIDE (Writing it down as he listens) You can see I'm awfully busy, Barrett, so what is it you want?

BARRETT Shouldn't the captain know about that iceberg, then?

BRIDE Not to worry, I already sent him half-dozen warnings just like it. If you ask me, they don't know what the bloody hell they're doing up there, excuse my French. It's like we say in the telegraphy business: "You can't be a radio operator and remain a Christian."

BARRETT So how much would it cost to send a message to my girl in England? Sort of a romantic message—

    (He shows Bride a small photo.)

BRIDE Very pretty. But romantic or not, minimum rate's 2 pounds, 4 pence.

'Ere! What's that you're doin'?

BRIDE   "Darlene Watkins, Billsthorp, Nottinghampshire." So what's the rest of it?

BARRETT   I don't know. It's got to be just the right thing. Darlene's sort of funny, y'see—she said if I wouldn't take her serious she knew somebody who would. And I'm not due back for almost two weeks yet. So I might as well come straight out with it—

(As he dictates his message, Bride will set about tapping it out.)

I'll be coming back to you, Darlene
Back to your dark eyes and hair
Marry me when I return, Darlene
And until that day my love, take care
Be thee well
May the Lord who watches all watch over thee
May God's heaven be your blanket as you softly sleep
Marry me
When you're fin'ly in my arms you'll plainly see
This devoted sailor's heart and soul
Are yours to keep!

BRIDE
Yours—to keep ...

(He stops and reflects)

Every day from G-M-O-M
"Good morning, old man"
To G-N-O-M
"Good night, old man"
My telegraph sends its messages to ships at sea . . .

Sending out its dit-dah-dit dah-dit . . .
Dit dit-dah-dit dah-dit
Dit dit-dah-dit dah-dit . . .

I was young and shy, detached and sad
Spent my days indoors, a home-bound lad
Hardly spoke, few friends
I kept myself to myself
Quite alone

Then I found Marconi's telegraph
It could span the planet's width by half
Fifty yards, two thousand miles
The same!
Touch the spark . . .sound the tone

And the night was alive
With a thousand voices
Fighting to be heard
And each and ev'ry one of them
connected to me ...

And my life came alive
With a thousand voices

Tapping out each word
Like a thousand people
Joined with a single heartbeat

Tapping out our dit dit-dah-dit dah-dit
Dit dit-dah-dit dah-dit

BARRETT   *Two bloody quid?* That's twice what they pay me to America 'n' back!

BRIDE   Hold on—maybe I could give you a professional discount.

BARRETT   Yeah? What'd *that* cost?

BRIDE   (Calculates, then:)   Nothing, they'll never know the difference.

BARRETT   Ta very much. You must be a romantic sort of person yourself.

BRIDE   Not me. Romance and telegraphy don't mix, see? How can you communicate with only one person when you've got the entire world talking to you? I'll need her name and address—

BARRETT   Darlene Watkins, Billsthorp, Nottinghampshire.

(As Bride starts tapping out message)

Dit dit-da-dit-dah
Everywhere . . .

BARRETT
Marry me

May the lord who watches all
Watch over thee

Marry me

May God's Heaven be your blanket
As you softly sleep

Marry me ...
  Marry me ...

Marry me!

BARRETT —Signed "Fred"

(He taps out "F-R-E-D" [dit-dit-dah-dit, dit-dah-dit, dit, dah-dit-dit] on his key)

BRIDE
Everywhere!

(He receives a signal from the receiver)

Message received.

(Lights fade; the scene changes to:)

S C E N E 8

The UPPER PROMENADE ("A") DECK

Then THE BOAT DECK

AT RISE: "Sunday morning, April 14" is displayed. Several of

BRIDE

It's alive with a thousand
voices

And ev'ry one of them
Connected to me
So alive with a thousand
voices

Those people
Joined with a single heartbeat
Tapping out our
Dit dit-dah-dit-dah-dit
Dit dit-dah-dit-dah-dit

Dit dit-dah-dit-dah

the 1st class passengers enter—the Astors, Thayers & son, Wideners, Guggenheim & Mme. Aubert and others, Capt. Smith arrives to lead their Sunday morning recessional.

CAPT. SMITH Ladies and gentlemen, after our Sunday service, all 1st Class Passengers are invited to the Boat Deck where our Bandmaster, Mr. Wallace Hartley, and his ensemble will be playing out-of-doors for your entertainment. And now we will conclude our service with Hymn number 27: "God Lift Me Up."

PASSENGERS
God lift me up in mighty waters
Keep my eyes on things above
Righteousness, divine atonement
Peace and everlasting love . . .

(The scene changes to: THE BOAT DECK: Bandmaster Hartley and his two-man ensemble greet the passengers)

HARTLEY Ladies and gentlemen—

(Playing the violin, he and the other musicians launch into a lively tune, played in ragtime)

Everyone up and out
Follow the band and shout: BAND
"Isn't it a lovely day?"   Yes!

HARTLEY
Watching all the ladies in Parisian fashion
On display

BAND
Young Mister Hartley is
Playing quite smartly
In rhythm that could never lag
It's a musical treat
To hear a band with a beat
Performing their latest rag!

HARTLEY

> (Greeting individual passengers)

> *How do you do, my friend?*
> *So good to see you once more!*
> *How long since we first met?*
> *Has it been three days or four?*
> *It seems like so much longer*
> *Than a little weekend jag*

BAND

> *On the ship, by ourselves*
> *On this glorious afternoon*
> *Doing the latest rag!*

HARTLEY

> *I love the cool of the breeze*
> *Feel the rhythm of the song in your knees*
> *Promenading along at your ease*
> *Like a feather in the air*

HARTLEY & BAND

> *Is that a hint of a chill?*
> *When you're dancing out of doors it's a thrill*
> *Keeps you hardy and healthier still*
> *Take a partner if you dare*

> *Everyone is bursting with emotion*
> *Dancing as we cross the mighty ocean*
> *Moving to the rhythm of*
> *The latest rag!*

ALL

> *Come on and*

MEN & BAND	**WOMEN**
Dance with me please	*Dance*
Feel the rhythm	
Of the song in your knees	*The latest ragtime*
Promenading along	
At your ease	*Ragtime*
Like a feather in the air!	*Now!*
Is that a hint of a chill?	*Dance*
When you're dancing	*The latest ragtime*
out of doors	
It's a thrill	
Keeps you hardy and	
Healthier still	*Ragtime*
Take a partner if you dare . . .	

ETCHES Ladies and gentlemen, the DaMicos!

> (A DANCE SECTION: Two professional dancers, the DaMicos, will perform, then show the passengers the steps for them to copy. Alice Beane, a 2nd Class interloper, attempts to join in but she keeps running into Etches who tries to chuck her out)

HARTLEY & BAND

> *Out on the well-deck*
> *Ship's personnel deck*
> *Feel all the ocean spray*

BAND

> *Get yourself upon*

HARTLEY & BAND

> *The upper hotel deck*
> *Oh what a swell deck!*
> *Great for your déjeuner*

BAND

Turn the corner on

BAND & HARTLEY	PASSENGERS
The port parallel deck	Port
It's la plus belle deck	
All of the rest passé	

ALL

Now the band is betting
This ragtime setting
Will take you away ...

Everyone up and out!
Nobody lag about
Let your darker spirits climb!
Strolling with the orchestra beside you
Playing four-four time

HARTLEY & HITCHENS

We've got a fellow
Who's better on cello
Than any other ship can brag

BAND

So take your girl by the hand
And lend an ear to the band
And do today's latest rag!

ALL

Come dancing!

HARTLEY, BAND & BYSTANDERS	DANCERS
Out on the well-deck	Out
Ship's personnel deck	
Feel all the ocean spray	

BAND

Get yourself upon

HARTLEY, BAND & BYSTANDERS	DANCERS
The upper hotel deck	Out
Oh what a swell deck!	
Kick all your troubles away	

BAND	DANCERS
Turn the corner on	
The port parallel deck	Out
Great demoiselle deck!	
Watch all the girls sashay	

ALL

How the ragtime music
The ragtime music
Can take you away!

(Split chorus)

Out on the well-deck	Dance with me please
Ship's personnel deck	Feel the rhythm of the song
Feel all the ocean spray	In your knees
	Promenading along
Upper hotel deck	At your ease
Oh what a swell deck!	Like a feather in the air
Kick all your troubles away	Is that a
The port parallel deck	Hint of a chill?
It's la plus belle deck	When you're dancing

All of the rest, passé	Out of doors
	It's a thrill!
	Keeps you hardy
Great demoiselle deck	And healthier still
Watch all the girls sashay!	Take a partner if you
dare!	

ALL

Everyone is bursting with emotion
Dancing as we cross the mighty ocean
Hasn't it been absolutely great to dance
The latest rag!

(The scene changes back to "A" DECK, 1ST CLASS PROMENADE; "Sunday Afternoon/April 14" is displayed. Everyone except Alice Beane has gone. Then Edgar Beane enters)

EDGAR BEANE Alice! I've been looking for you everywhere. You're not supposed to be here. What've you been up to?

ALICE BEANE (Proud of herself) Afternoon dancing.

EDGAR BEANE Afternoon dancing?

ALICE BEANE It's what they call a "thé-dansant."

EDGAR BEANE Back home it's what they call a crock of—

ALICE BEANE (Quickly) Language, Edgar!

EDGAR BEANE Come on, little girl. I don't really think we belong here—

ALICE BEANE Oh, applesauce, Edgar!

I have danced with the first class. Edgar
It was oh, such a dream come true!

EDGAR BEANE

That class isn't for our kind, Alice . . .

ALICE BEANE

That won't do!

Haven't you noticed, Edgar? These days nobody's any better than anybody else! Take the Wideners of Philadelphia—I stood right next to them, Edgar! They have this extremely handsome son, Harry, the Harvard man. I'll tell you the God's honest truth, Edgar—I'd let that boy marry our Lucy in a *second*.

EDGAR BEANE Well, that's half the battle.

ALICE BEANE You can make fun all you want, Edgar, but I want more out of life than Indianapolis, Indiana.

EDGAR BEANE But that's why I arranged this trip, Alice—to show you the world.

ALICE BEANE I don't want to see the world, Edgar! There are too many other places I'd rather see first!

There are hotels on islands, Edgar!
Great resorts near a sandy beach . . .

EDGAR BEANE

That's a world that's beyond our income
and our reach . . .

ALICE BEANE That's because you've always been satis-

fied with only one dinky little hardware store instead of branching out. How do you think those millionaires got all their millions, Edgar?

EDGAR BEANE Why don't you just calm down, Alice, and enjoy what we have?

ALICE BEANE
*Please don't tell me never
I'll want this forever . . . ever . . . .*

There's a new world around us, Edgar

EDGAR BEANE
Won't you ever give up that view?

ALICE BEANE
*I want more than we've got now, Edgar
Why don't you?*

EDGAR BEANE I don't know. What do you suggest we do about it, Alice?

ALICE BEANE I don't know. I'm going for a walk now, Edgar. I have to be alone for a while—

(She goes. At a loss, he exits the other side of the stage, as the scene changes to:)

SCENE 9

THE BRIDGE; Then THE PROMENADE ("B"), THE SALOON ("D") AND THE MIDDLE ("F") DECKS; the 1ST CLASS SMOKE ROOM; THE BOAT DECK; THE CROW'S NEST; and the AFTER DECK.

AT RISE: "Ship's Bridge; Sunday Evening/April 14" is displayed. On the bridge: Murdoch, and, at the helm, Hitchens. As Six Bells rings, Lightoller, holding a radiogram, enters.

LIGHTOLLER Three bells, Mr. Murdoch.

MURDOCH Thank you, Mr. Lightoller. Hold your course, quartermaster—west, northwest, 2-9-2 degrees.

HITCHENS West, northwest, 2-9-2 degrees, aye, sir.

(Capt. Smith enters)

CAPT. SMITH Mr. Murdoch, what's our present speed?

MURDOCH Steady at 22 knots, sir.

CAPT. SMITH Have there been any reports of mechanical difficulty since reaching that speed?

MURDOCH No, sir. None at all.

CAPT. SMITH Very good. Increase speed to 23 knots.

LIGHTOLLER Captain, there's been another ice warning, sir. *Mesaba* reports a large berg at 42 degrees north.

(He hands him the radiogram)

CAPT. SMITH 42 degrees. That's in total agreement with all of the other reports we've received. Excpet for this one, from the French liner, *La Touraine*—"41 degrees."—now that puts it a good deal closer, doesn't it. How do you explain the difference?

MURDOCH It must have been an error in transmission, sir.

CAPT. SMITH The radio—I'll never accept the damn thing.

LIGHTOLLER I'm afraid it's here to stay, sir.

CAPT. SMITH Which means we'll soon be taking our orders from safe, dry little offices on shore.

LIGHTOLLER It's a brand new world, Captain.

CAPT. SMITH Thank God I won't be around to see it. 23 knots, Mr. Murdoch.

MURDOCH 23 knots, yes, sir.

(He goes to the phone)

Engine room—increase speed to 81 revolutions of the wing propellers, Mr. Bell.

("'B' Deck; 1st Class" is displayed. Isidor and Ida Straus are standing at the rail)

IDA STRAUS I'm still waiting, Mr. Straus—

ISIDOR STRAUS For what?

IDA STRAUS The reason you sent our son Jesse a radio message.

ISIDOR STRAUS He and his cousin Nathan want to make Macy's the largest retail store in the world. They even want to give away catalogs, like Sears and Roebuck. It's totally crazy!

IDA STRAUS What did you tell him?

ISIDOR STRAUS To go ahead! It's a new world out there, Mrs. Straus. I don't pretend to understand it.

("'D' Deck; 2nd Class" is displayed; Edgar Beane, clearly very depressed, is alone, his chin on the rail. Etches now enters and stands next to him, smoking a cigarette, he glances at him.)

ETCHES Good evening, sir. Henry Etches, 1st Class Steward.

EDGAR BEANE (Without any enthusiasm) Edgar Beane, 2nd Class passenger.

ETCHES Beane—I know that name—

EDGAR BEANE You probably ran into my wife. She likes dancing with millionaires.

ETCHES (Placing her) Ah. Yes, quite so, sir. My condolences.

("'F' Deck; 3rd Class" is displayed. Kate McGowan and Jim Farrell stand at the rail)

JIM FARRELL That's a far-off look I'm seein' in your eye, Kate—which far-off place is it you're lookin' at? America? Or Ireland.

KATE McGOWAN (A beat) If you must know, I was thinkin' about a friend of mine—a very dear friend. It seems she left home because she'd made a mistake. A mistake she couldn't get rid of.

JIM FARRELL She shoulda been more careful.

(1st Class Deck:)

IDA STRAUS So what are you going to do with the rest of your life?

ISIDOR STRAUS Who knows? Maybe run for Congress again. I'll tell you the truth—I really liked it there. And the best part is, you don't have to know anything.

(2nd Class deck:)

EDGAR BEANE It seems she wants more out of life than I can give her.

ETCHES Isn't that always the way, sir.

(A beat)

I had a wife once—

EDGAR BEANE What happened?

ETCHES Nothing. I still have her.

(Looking at the sea)

In all my years I never saw it so calm.

EDGAR BEANE Is it my imagination or are we going faster than ever before?

(3rd Class Deck:)

KATE McGOWAN If my friend were here instead of me, Jim, what would you say to her?

JIM FARRELL Well, I'd say—what would I call her, then?

KATE McGOWAN We're all named Kate, you know that.

JIM FARRELL So I'd say—"Kate, do you know who the father is?"

KATE McGOWAN What a sad question! What d'ye take her for?

JIM FARRELL And he refused to go with her? Decent work bein' hard to find he probably didn't want to leave his job.

KATE McGOWAN Or his wife. So tell me, Jim Farrell, could a decent feller care for a woman who already had a bit of family?

(BELOW: "1st Class/Smoke Room" is displayed; Four Bells rings. At game tables, bridge and other card games are being played by men only, all smoking cigars. Upstage: a miniature replica of *R.M.S. Titanic* on the mantle. [The same one seen in the Prologue.] Just completing a hand of bridge at the center table: George Widener partnered with J. H. Rogers, a bespectacled American in his 40s; their opponents are J. J. Astor and the Major. Sitting at another table playing are Benj. Guggenheim and John Thayer. The bellboy will pass through from time to time offering cigars and brandy.)

THE MAJOR (To Rogers) Oh, well made, sir! Astor, that'll cost us some.

J. J. ASTOR It's your deal, Major. Mr. Rogers—your reputation as a fine bridge-player is well-earned. You play an *excellent* game.

J. H. ROGERS   Thank you, sir.

J. J. ASTOR   Either that or you're uncommonly lucky.

J. H. ROGERS   Bridge isn't a game of chance, Mr. Astor.

THE MAJOR   Reminds me of the time I was playing bridge with Lord Raglan during the Crimean campaign when, out of nowhere came 2,000—

EVERYONE   —*crazed godless savages!*

JOHN THAYER   I've been told on very good authority that there are professional gamblers on board, card sharpers who actually make their living traveling back and forth across the Atlantic.

THE MAJOR   (He laughs)   Gamblers? Nonsense! How do these rumors start?

J. H. ROGERS   Oh, you can be sure they're here, Major. How could they pass up the opportunity of fleecing a passenger list like this one? I've even heard talk that the notorious Jay Yates is aboard.

JOHN THAYER   I don't remember seeing *his* name on the passenger list—

J. H. ROGERS   Well, you wouldn't, would you? But I'll give you ten to one he's here somewhere.

(The CROW'S NEST, equipped with a brass bell and telephone; "Crow's Nest" is displayed. Five Bells sound as Lookout Frederick Fleet scans the sea)

FLEET
No moon
No wind
Nothing to spy things by
No wave
No swell
No line where sea meets sky
Stillness
Darkness
Can't see a thing, says I
No reflection
Not a shadow
Not a glint of light
Meets the eye . . .

And we go sailing
Sailing
Ever westward on the sea
We go sailing
Sailing

Ever on
Go we . . .

(On the 1ST CLASS DECK: Isidor and Ida Straus,
as before)

IDA STRAUS
It's a beautiful night, Mr. Straus
Even though there's no moon
Look at all the stars
Can you find the Big Dipper?

ISIDOR STRAUS   The Big Dipper? I can't even find our
own stateroom. Every time I go out for a walk, finding my
way back is an adventure.

IDA STRAUS
Maye you should drop bread crumbs

ISIDOR STRAUS
Can you feel how cold it's getting, Mrs. Straus?
All in the past couple of hours
Would you like me to get your fur stole?

IDA STRAUS   What, and maybe never see you again?

No thank you, I'd rather freeze

(On the 3RD CLASS DECK: Kate McGowan and
Jim Farrell)

JIM FARRELL
Are you cold, then, Katie?

KATE McGOWAN
Not now that you've got your arm around me . . .

JIM FARRELL But I don't—

(Realizing, he puts his arm around her)

You're a funny one, Kate McGowan.

KATE McGOWAN   T'anks very much.

JIM FARRELL   Because you come right out with what you
want.

KATE McGOWAN   And you find that funny, do you?

What kind of girl do you think I am?
You think I need to be told what I want?
Life's too short for that, my boy-o

(ON THE BRIDGE: Capt. Smith and Lightoller
regard the sea ahead; Hitchens is at the helm;
Murdoch reads dispatches posted on a board)

CAPT. SMITH
The weather's quite changed, Mr. Lightoller

LIGHTOLLER
Yes, sir, it's turned very cold

Only one point above freezing.

MURDOCH
Ocean temp'rature's down to thirty-one degrees,
Captain

CAPT. SMITH   Warn the carpenter to check our supply of
fresh water, Mr. Murdoch—and tell the engine room to
watch the steam winches.

MURDOCH
Aye, aye, sir

(He goes to the phone)

CAPT. SMITH
There's not much wind, is there?

LIGHTOLLER
No, sir. It appears to be a flat calm

(The CROW'S NEST: Fleet sings counterpoint, alternating with Smith and Lightoller:)

FLEET

. . . And we go sailing
Sailing
Ever westward on the sea

. . . We go sailing
Sailing

SMITH, LIGHTOLLER & MURDOCH

See how calm it is
Smooth as polished glass
Ah, the open sea
Feel the bite in the air
Ah the open sea
Smooth as polished glass

FLEET

Ever on
Go we . . .

CAPT. SMITH   Good night, gentlemen. I'll be just inside. Keep a sharp watch. The naked eye, that's something you can depend on.

LIGHTOLLER   Good night, sir.

CAPT. SMITH   Good night.

(He goes)

LIGHTOLLER (Picks up the telephone)   Crow's nest, this is the bridge. Keep an eye peeled for ice.

(Charles Clarke and Caroline Neville have arrived and now share the 2ND CLASS DECK with Etches and Edgar Beane)

CAROLINE NEVILLE

Charles, think!
In two days, America!

What's the first thing you're going to do when we get there, darling? After marrying me, of course.

CHARLES CLARKE   Apply to the sports desk of an important New York newspaper. I'm sure they can use a journalist with my experience.

CAROLINE NEVILLE   But you don't know anything about American sports, do you, darling?

CHARLES CLARKE   It's not so terribly complicated, really. Their football is similar to our rugger, you see—except for some reason their chaps need to wear a great deal of padding.

CAROLINE NEVILLE   They sound like an eminently sensible race.

CHARLES CLARKE
Let us both hope so . . .

BOTH
That's why we're going there.

(The 1ST CLASS SMOKE ROOM: Astor, Widener, the Major and Rogers are still playing, their cigars producing clouds of smoke. As Wallace Hartley, at the piano, begins playing a waltz ["Autumn"], Mrs. Charlotte Cardoza enters. All heads turn, surprised.)

MRS. CARDOZA   Good evening, gentlemen.

THE MAJOR   Madam, this happens to be the Smoke Room!

MRS. CARDOZA (Coughing and waving the smoke away)   So I see.

J. J. ASTOR   Women are never permitted in the 1st Class Smoking Room, madam.

MRS. CARDOZA   Don't look so shocked, gentlemen. There's a new world out there.

THE MAJOR (Looking around)   There's a new world out where?

MRS. CARDOZA   Mr. Hartley, that's a new melody—what's it called?

WALLACE HARTLEY   "Autumn," ma'am.
Autumn
Shall we meet in the autumn?
Golden and glowing by autumn
Shall we still be best of friends?
Best of friends . . .

MRS. CARDOZA   Gentlemen—let me introduce myself—

J. J. ASTOR   Mrs. Charlotte Cardoza. I know who you are, madam. Recently widowed with a *considerably* generous inheritance.

MRS. CARDOZA   And I know about you, Mr. Astor. Recently remarried to a *considerably* younger wife.

J. J. ASTOR   You seem to enjoy shocking people, madam. I have heard you described as "a modern woman" by people who don't mean it as a compliment.

MRS. CARDOZA   And I've heard you described as "the world's greatest monument to unearned income."

WALLACE HARTLEY
. . . Let breezes blow
And turn cold
As we continue growing old
This autumn
Love newly found
May yet last

MRS. CARDOZA   So what do you say, gentlemen? I happen to play an excellent game of auction bridge—may I join you?

THE MAJOR   Where's your sense of occasion, madam? I understand you've just lost your husband.

MRS. CARDOZA   Yes. But not at cards.

(As the Major leaves in disgust, Astor offers her his place at the table and smiling, she sits.)

And another thing—would you mind putting out those dreadful cigars?

(The 3RD CLASS DECK: Kate McGowan and Jim Farrell)

JIM FARRELL   So, Kate McGowan, what immodest thing are you going to say to me next, then?

KATE McGOWAN   I'm going to say: "Jim Farrell, will you marry me?"

JIM FARRELL   For the love of God, Kate! I know it's the New World we're goin' to, but we haven't got there yet. Don't you leave *nothin'* for the man to say?

KATE McGOWAN   He can say "yes!" We're gonna need each other when we get there, me boy-o, and me baby's gonna need a da, so we'd better settle it right now. Will you say "yes," then?

JIM FARRELL   Well, I might as well! Chances are you wouldn't take a "no," anyway!

(A pause)

Well, Kate? Aren't you going to throw me down and kiss me?

(In the CROW'S NEST:)

FLEET
Ahead we plow
Into the dark'ning night
Can't see the bow
How then to search
With only starlight? . . .

(As the song continues, the scene changes to: THE PROW OF THE BOAT DECK. The company is assembled as the ship's personnel—crew and staff—join the passengers, singing counterpoint:)

FLEET AND PERSONNEL	PASSENGERS
No moon	*Autumn*
No wind	*Shall we all meet in the*
Nothing to spy things	*Autumn*
By	*Golden and glowing, by*
No wave	*Autumn*
No swell	*Shall we still be best of*
	Friends
No line where sea	
Meets sky	*Best of friends?*

ALL
Stillness, darkness
Can't see a thing, says I
No reflection
Not a shadow

Not a glint of light
Meets the eye

PASSENGERS
And we go sailing
Sailing
Ever westward
On the sea . . .
We go sailing
Sailing

FLEET AND PERSONNEL
See how calm it is
Smooth as polished glass
Ah, the open sea
Feel the bite in the air
Ah, the open sea
Smooth as polished glass

ALL
Ever on
Go we . . .

FLEET
No moon
No wind . . .

(With passengers)

No moon
No wind

FLEET	**BRIDE**
No moon	*The night was alive*
No wind	*With a thousand voices . . .*
No moon	*Night was alive*
No wind	*With a thousand voices*

	BARRETT
No moon	*The screws were turning*
No wind	*At eighty-one*
No moon	*The screws were turning*
No wind	*At eighty-one*

	BRIDE	**BARRETT**
No moon	*The night was alive*	*The screws were turning*
No wind	*With a thousand voices*	*At eighty-one*

	BRIDE	**BARRETT**	**ANDREWS**
No moon	*Night was alive*	*The screws were*	*At once a poem*
		Turning	*And the perfection*
No wind	*With a thousand Voices*	*At eighty-one*	*Of physical Engineering*

(In the CROW'S NEST: Fleet sees something straight ahead)

FLEET   Dear Mother of God—

(He rings the brass bell three times—Ding! Ding! Ding!—then cranks the telephone)

Iceberg right ahead!

(Murdoch, Lightoller and Hitchens though downstage are on the "Bridge." They will remain remarkably calm.)

MURDOCH   Thank you. Quartermaster, hard a'starboard.

HITCHENS   Hard a'starboard. The helm's hard over, sir.

MURDOCH   Engines, full astern.

LIGHTOLLER   Full astern, sir—

HITCHENS   The bow's reacting, Mr. Murdoch—two degrees to port.

MURDOCH   The distance, Mr. Fleet—

FLEET   A quarter mile—maybe a little less—

HITCHENS   —nine degrees—ten, eleven, a full point—

MURDOCH   (To himself)   Turn—turn—

HITCHENS   Jesus, Mary and Joseph. Look at the size of it—

LIGHTOLLER   Looks like the Rock of bloody Gibraltar—

HITCHENS   It's going to pass a'starboard, sir—

MURDOCH   Yes, it's all right, I think we're going to miss it.

(BLACKOUT)

SCENE 10

THE COLLISION; A TABLEAU.

Titanic, looking quite small and insignificant as, under a star-lit but moonless sky, she sails across the dark, smooth-as-glass sea, lights ablaze.

"Lat. 41' 44" North/Long. 50' 24" West; 11:40 pm." is displayed.

As she continues off, there's a loud, ominous scraping sound; it lasts for a full eight seconds.

FIRST ACT CURTAIN

1069

ACT TWO

(After the ENTR'ACTE:)

ACT TWO

SCENE 1

1ST, 2ND & 3RD CLASS CORRIDORS, & THE BRIDGE.

A corridor on the Upper Promenade ("A") Deck: a line of 1st Class cabin doors.

AT RISE: "Lat. 41' 44" North Long. 50' 24" West; 11:47 pm" is displayed. The corridor is deserted; there is total silence. Then, one of the cabin doors opens and Benjamin Guggenheim appears. He looks around, then moves to the next cabin door and knocks.

BENJ. GUGGENHEIM   George—George, are you there?—Wake up, George—

    (The door opens and George Widener peeks out; he is wearing a bathrobe.)

WIDENER   Who is it? Benjamin! What's wrong? It's nearly midnight.

BENJ. GUGGENHEIM   George—do you hear anything?

WIDENER   Hear anything?

    (He listens)

No. Nothing.

BENJ. GUGGENHEIM   That's the point. The engines have stopped.

WIDENER   Stopped?

    (Listening again)

By God, I think you're right.

    (1st Class Steward Etches enters, stops at the first door and knocks.)

ETCHES   Wake up, wake up—

BENJ. GUGGENHEIM   Mr. Etches—why have we stopped?

ETCHES   I couldn't say, Mr. Guggenheim, but I don't suppose it's anything much.

MADELEINE ASTOR   (Dressed in her peignoir; she opens the door to face Etches)   Mr. Etches—is something wrong?

ETCHES   I don't think so, madam. Just following orders—

    (He moves on to another door and knocks)

Wake up—wake up—

    (ON THE BRIDGE: Murdoch is at the helm as Lightoller enters)

LIGHTOLLER   We grazed it below the water line on the starboard side—

MURDOCH   (He appears to be in shock)   How bad is it, then?

LIGHTOLLER   I don't know yet—

    (On the telephone)

All stations! Damage report!

    (To Murdoch)

The exact time of contact was 11:40 pm. One of us should enter it in the log—

MURDOCH   If we only grazed it, it couldn't be that bad—

LIGHTOLLER   Then we've nothing to worry about, have we?

    (Capt. Smith enters buttoning his tunic)

CAPT. SMITH   Report, Mr. Murdoch—

    (When Murdoch doesn't answer, Lightoller steps in)

LIGHTOLLER   We've struck an iceberg, sir—Starboard side. We don't yet know the extent of the damage but I've taken the liberty of rousing the passengers.

CAPT. SMITH   I want them on deck and wearing life preservers. At the very least they could use a drill. We've never had one, have we?

    (IN THE 1ST CLASS CORRIDOR: Etches and two stewards are knocking at the doors; more cabin doors will open, one by one, and other 1st-class passengers emerge—Isidor & Ida Straus, Eleanor Widener, Mme. Aubert, Marion Thayer, Mrs. Cardoza and the Major—most wearing nightgowns and robes)

ETCHES & STEWARDS
Wake up! Wake up! Wake up!
Wake up! Wake up!

   (Knock-knock-knock)

Wake up! Wake up! Wake up!
Wake up! Wake up!

   (Knock-knock-knock)

Wake up! Wake up! Wake up!
Wake up! Wake up!

   (Knock-knock-knock)

Wake up! Wake up! Wake up!
Wake up! Wake up!

   (Knock-knock-knock)

STEWARD
First Class passengers
Proceed at once to the salon
Please bring your life preservers and
Await further instructions!

ALL FIRST CLASS PASSENGERS
Almost midnight
Strange commotion   **ETCHES & STEWARDS**
In the corridor   *Wake up! Wake up! Wake*
                            up!
                            Wake up! Wake up!
Engine noise
Appears much quieter
Than it was before   *Wake up! Wake up!Wake*
                            up!
                            Wake up!Wake up! . . .
Can there be some incident
Some accident

ALL
The captain can't ignore? . . .

JOHN THAYER (Enters holding a large chunk of ice)
George, look what I found on deck. There must be a ton
of It—

GEORGE WIDENER   Be a sport, John, and chip off a
piece for my drink.

ETCHES   Ladies and Gentlemen, the captain would be
most grateful if you would proceed to the Grand Salon.
And please dress warmly.

   (On the BRIDGE: Lightoller is hanging up the
   telephone; he turns to Capt Smith)

LIGHTOLLER   We're taking water in boiler rooms 4, 5
and 6, sir. In 6, the water's already up to their knees.

CAPT. SMITH   Close the watertight doors, Mr. Lightoller,
and see that the pumps are activated. Then rouse the
carpenter and have him sound the ship.

LIGHTOLLER   It's all done, sir—

CAPT. SMITH   Our position, Mr. Murdoch?

   (As Murdoch seems not to have heard, his
   hands glued to the helm)

Mr. Murdoch! *Our position!—*

LIGHTOLLER (Stepping in and checking the chart)
Latitude 41 degrees 44 minutes north, Longitude 50
degrees 24 minutes west, sir!

CAPT. SMITH   Inform the radio room. For God's sake,
Mr. Murdoch! Let go of the helm, we're dead in the
water!

MURDOCH (Stepping back, still in a daze)   I'm sorry,
sir—

   (2nd Class Corridor: Less opulent; "2nd Class
   Corridor; 11:53 pm." is displayed. A bellboy
   crosses, calling through a megaphone:)

STEWARD
Second Class passengers
Proceed to the First Class Salon
Please bring your life preservers
And await further instructions.

   (2nd-class stewards begin knocking on doors;
   2nd-class passengers will appear, among them
   Charles Clarke & Caroline Neville and Edgar
   & Alice Beane)

2ND CLASS PASSENGERS
What's happened?
Do YOU know?
It seems the ship is stopping
Have you heard?
Do you know?
I vaguely heard a rumor
An impact
Slight impact
I vaguely heard a rumor
What's happened?

2ND CLASS STEWARD   I understand an iceberg scratched some of her new paint and the captain doesn't want to go on until she's fixed up good as new.

CAROLINE NEVILLE   Well, I think I'll stay in cabin and finish my book—

2ND CLASS STEWARD   I'm afraid you'll have to go to the 1st Class Grand Salon right away, madam—captain's orders.

EDGAR BEANE   Come along, Alice, here's your chance to mingle with the swells.

2ND CLASS STEWARD   Please, you must get your life preservers right away. There's no time to lose.

ALICE BEANE   I can't go up there looking like this? I've got to fix my face.

EDGAR BEANE   The *ship* will be fixed before that, Alice—

(On the BRIDGE: Ismay enters)

ISMAY   E. J.! Why have we stopped? I want an immediate explanation.

Do you know?
It seems the ship is stopping

Get up now
Get dressed now
Put on your warmest clothing
What's happened?
Do YOU know?
It seems the ship is stopping

A rumor
A rumor
I vaguely heard a rumor
An impact
Slight impact
It seems the ship is stopping

SPLIT CHORUS		STEWARDS
Can there be	*Is there*	*There is*
Some incident	*An incident*	*No incident*
Some—	*Is there an—*	*There is no*

ALL
  —Accident the captain can't ignore?

CHARLES CLARKE   Steward—why has the ship stopped?

CAPT. SMITH   We've struck an iceberg, Mr. Ismay.

ISMAY   That was pretty damned careless, wasn't it?

CAPT. SMITH   We're trying to assess the damage, sir.

ISMAY   Damage? What damage?

CAPT. SMITH   We're taking on water in the boiler rooms but we've closed the emergency doors and I'm quite certain that everything is under control.

ISMAY   Then I trust you'll have us underway as soon as possible.

CAPT. SMITH   Mr. Andrews is making a complete inspection. If you'll just be patient, sir, you'll have his report the moment it's available.

ISMAY   In the meantime, captain, I see no need to alarm the passengers.

(3rd Class Corridor: This one quite bare; "3rd Class Corridor 11:56 pm" is displayed. 3rd-class stewards, a less refined lot, appear and begin banging loudly and rudely on the doors.)

STEWARD
Third Class passengers
Fore and abaft of the well deck
Please find your life preservers
And await further instructions

(3rd-class passengers, including the three Kates and Jim Farrell, have appeared at their doors; some speak in foreign languages.)

KATE MURPHEY   What is it? What's goin' on?

KATE McGOWAN   There was this terrible scrapin' noise and then we just stopped.

KATE MULLINS   What're we s'posed to do now?

JIM FARRELL   I'm goin' upstairs and have a look—

3RD CLASS STEWARD   You'll wait down here like you're told!

3RD CLASS PASSENGERS & STEWARDS

(Split chorus)
What's happened?   Almost midnight
Do YOU know?
It seems the ship is stopping!
Have YOU heard?   Strange commotion
Do YOU know?
I vaguely heard a rumor . . .

An impact   In the corridor . . .
Slight impact
I vaguely heard a rumor
What's happened?
Do YOU know?
It seems the ship is stopping!

Get up now!   Engine noise
Get dressed now!
Put on your warmest clothing!
What's happened?   Appears much quieter
Do YOU know?
It seems the ship is stopping!

A rumor
A rumor
I vaguely heard a rumor
An impact
Slight impact
It seems the ship is stopping

Than it was before . . .

ALL PASSENGERS	STEWARDS
Can there be	*There is*
Some incident	*No incident*
Some accident	*There is no accident*
The captain	*The captain*
Can't ignore	*Will ignore*

(On the BRIDGE: Andrews enters)

CAPT. SMITH   Yes, Mr. Andrews?

ANDREWS (Reading from his notebook)   There's a series of small gashes below the water line stretching 300 feet along her starboard side—there's water in the forepeak—in the number 1, 2 and 3 holds—in the mail room—and in 3 of the boiler rooms. In all, 6 of her 16 compartments have been breached.

ISMAY But that's all right. You assured us those compartments are watertight.

ANDREWS   She was designed to stay afloat with any 3 flooded. Perhaps even 4. But certainly not 6.

ISMAY   Andrews—what are you saying?

ANDREWS   Titanic is sinking, Mr. Ismay.

ISMAY   Nonsense! God Himself couldn't sink this ship!

CAPT. SMITH   How long has she got, Mr. Andrews?

ANDREWS (A beat)   An hour and a half, Captain. Two at the most.

(There is total silence. Lights fade as the scene changes to:)

SCENE 2

THE UPPER PROMENADE ("A") DECK:

THE 1ST CLASS GRAND SALON.

The elegant staircase descends, culminating, at the bottom, in a bronze statue of a winged angel holding an electric lamp.

AT RISE: "1st-Class Grand Salon; 12:03 am" is displayed. Lightoller enters, right, and crosses, meeting Etches who has entered left. Lightoller whispers the true condition of the ship, to Etches' surprise and dismay, then goes. As Etches ponders, the 1st-class passengers begin assembling—Astors, Strauses, Thayers, Wideners, Benj. Guggenheim & Mme. Aubert, and Mrs.Cardoza—variously dressed in dinner clothes as well as pajamas, nightgowns and bathrobes, some beneath furs and overcoats—all carrying their life preservers. They are curious, anxious and confused.

J. J. ASTOR & GEORGE WIDENER
    Strange and quite disorienting being here
    Recently awakened from a dream
    How the lights burn!
    Ev'ry crystal bright as a star!

BENJ. GUGGENHEIM & JOHN THAYER
Dressed in your pyjamas in the grand salon
Looks to be bizarre in the extreme
Things could improve if the steward opens the bar!

ALL FOUR
Oh . . . it's a mem'ry I'll want to keep!
Now . . . I would like to go
Back to sleep . . .

(Now the women join them)

1ST CLASS PASSENGERS
Dressed in your pyjamas in the Grand Salon
Wondering if things are what they seem
Can you be sure? Do you ever
Know where you are?

ETCHES   Ladies and gentlemen, could I have your attention, please! The captain would appreciate it if all of you were *wearing* your life preservers—

J.J. ASTOR   Mr. Etches! Over here, Mr. Etches!—

ETCHES   I'll be right with you, Mr. Astor—

GEORGE WIDENER   (Stopping him)   Please, Mr. Etches—what the devil's going on?

BENJ. GUGGENHEIM   Tell me straight, man—are we in any danger?

ETCHES   Danger, Mr. Guggenheim? On this ship?

Mr. Astor, please, your life-belt
Mr. Guggenheim, please put it on now
Captain's orders
Ladies and gentlemen, wear your life-belts . . .

ETCHES
Mrs. Widener, if you would, m'am
Mr. Thayer, we must insist now
It's a mere formality
There is no cause for concern

ETCHES & STEWARDESSES
We'll be on our way!
A minor delay now . . .
A simple precaution
A moment of rest

We'll be on our way!
We hardly need stay now . . .
In a moment or two she'll be right again
Travelling west!

JOHN THAYER   See here, Mr. Etches, I demand to know exactly what's happening!

ETCHES   The latest word, sir, seems to be that she's damaged one of the wing propellers and we could be delayed for an entire day, sir.

THAYER
I don't like the way this sounds . . .

BENJ. GUGGENHEIM
Not a bit, not a bit, not a little bit . . .

THAYER
We spent eighteen hundred pounds

GUGGENHEIM
Not a bit, not a bit, not a little bit . . .

GUGGENHEIM & THAYER
This is not the sort of a voyage we paid for!
I demand to know what the ship is delayed for!
Right now!

PASSENGERS, BELLBOY & STEWARDESSES
How could this ever have come to pass

ETCHES
Christ! look who's here!
It's the second class!

(Several 2nd-class passengers, including Charles Clarke & Caroline Neville and Edgar & Alice Beane, have entered and are looking around, impressed by their surroundings. Alice Beane only has eyes for the 1st-class passengers)

ALICE BEANE Edgar, look! What did I tell you? Everybody who's anybody!

EDGAR BEANE You're the only person here I don't recognize.

ALICE BEANE
Ev'rything is gorgeous in the grand salon!
Stunningly appointed for the cream
Thousands of bucks
Gets a trip deluxe without par!

ALL PASSENGERS
Dressed in your pyjamas
In the Grand Salon
Feels to be bizarre
In the extreme
How the lights burn
Ev'ry crystal bright
As a star

ETCHES & STEWARDS
Mr. Astor, please
Your life-belt
Mr. Guggenheim, please
Put it on now
It's a mere formality
There is no cause for
Concern

STEWARDS	1ST GROUP	2ND GROUP	3RD GROUP
We'll be on our way! A minor delay now A simple pre-caution! A moment of rest! We'll be on our way! We hardly need stay now	Strange and quite disorienting being here! Recently awakened in a daze! Ev'ry light is burning with intensity! Ev'rything surrounded by a haze! Strange and quite disorienting being here! Recently Awakened in a need . . .	We'll be on our way! A minor delay now! A simple precaution A moment of rest! We'll be on our way! We hardly need . . .	Strange and quite disorienting being here! Recently Awakened in a daze! Ev'ry light is burning with intensity! We'll be on our way! Strange and quite disori-enting being here!

(They all stop as the tea-cart begins rolling slowly across the Salon, the china rattling. All eyes are fixed on it. When it disappears off, the passengers continue, but hesitantly, with much less conviction:)

ETCHES
Mr. Guggenheim, please
Upstairs, now . . .
Mrs. Widener, if you would
Ma'am
It's a mere formality
There is no
Cause for concern

EVERYONE ELSE
Wondering if things are what
They seem . . .
Can you be sure?
Do you ever know where you
Are?

STEWARDS	1ST GROUP	2ND GROUP	3RD GROUP
We'll be on our way A minor delay now! A simple pre-caution! A moment of rest! We'll be on our way! We hardly need stay now	Strange and quite disorienting being here! Recently awakened in a daze! Ev'ry light is burning with intensity! Ev'rything surrounded by a haze! Strange and quite disorienting being here! Recently awakened in a daze	We'll be on our way! A minor delay now! A simple precaution A moment of rest! We'll be on our way! We hardly need stay now!	Strange and quite disorienting being here! Recently Awakened in a daze! Ev'ry light is burning with intensity! We'll be on our way! Strange and quite disorienting being here! Recently

*Any minute
now!*
    Any minute!
*Any minute
now!*
*Any minute
now!*
*Any minute
now!*
*Any minute
now!*

*awakened in
a
daze!*

*Any
minute!*

ALL
*We'll be on our way!
We'll be on our way!
We'll be on our way!
Our way!
Our way!*

(Lights fade as the scene changes to:)

SCENE 3

THE LOWER ("F") DECK, a 3rd-Class area.

(NOTE: The audience's perspective is from below, looking up a stairwell; the characters, looking straight out, will appear to be looking down.)

AT RISE: "'F' Deck/3rd-class Stairwell; 12:10 am" is displayed. The three Kates appear at the top of the stairs.

KATE McGOWAN
*Jim Farrell!
Are ya down there?
It's blocked up here, we can't get through!
What the hell are we supposed to do?
Jim Farrell, where've you gotten to?*

JIM FARRELL (entering)
*Over here, Kate! look here, Kate!
There's water runnin' on the floor!
See it comin' underneath the door!
And I think behind it there's lots more! . . .*

It's two foot deep in the men's dormitory. The boat's sinking!

KATE MURPHEY   What're we supposed to do, then—drown with all them other rats?

KATE McGOWAN Don't be daft—
*There's lifeboats!
They're up there!
I've seen 'em in a snapshot!*

KATE MULLINS
Me too, Kate!

KATE MURPHEY
Me three, Kate!

THREE KATES
*How the hell do we get up there!
How the hell do we get through that gate?
How long are we supposed to wait?
Who the hell is looking out for us?! . . .*

(Barrett appears)

BARRETT   What are you people doing here? Don't you know the ship's on her way down?

KATE McGOWAN   Who are you, then?

BARRETT   Frederick Barrett, stoker. We've gotta go up to the lifeboats—

JIM FARRELL   What do you think we're tryin' to do, man?

BARRETT   We're goners for sure if we can't get to those lifeboats—

JIM FARRELL   We'll have to find another way, all right—

KATE MURPHEY   What other way? I never seen no other way—

BARRETT   I know one. I snuck up to the radio room yesterday. And I didn't get caught, neither.

KATE MULLINS   How could such a terrible thing happen to such a marvelous ship?

KATE MURPHEY   Some marvelous ship—

BARRETT   Hurry up before we all drown!

KATE McGOWAN   You wait and see—we're gonna end up havin' to *swim* to America!

(The scene changes: There's the sound of the telegraph signalling its dots and dashes.)

SCENE 4

THE BOAT DECK; then THE RADIO ROOM.

AT RISE: "Boat Deck; 12:16 am" is displayed. Several 1st-class passengers—including the Astors, Wideners, Thayers, Benj. Guggenheim & Mme. Aubert, Charles & Caroline, Mrs. Cardoza & J. H. Rogers—cross the deck, on their way to the lifeboats.

ETCHES   Ladies and gentlemen. This way, please, we're headed for the Boat Deck—

EDGAR BEANE   Not so fast, Alice—

ALICE BEANE   Don't dawdle, Edgar—I want to make sure we're in the same lifeboat as the Astors—

MME. AUBERT   Benjamin, I am afraid.

BENJ. GUGGENHEIM   Relax, my dear—this ship could smash into a hundred icebergs and we wouldn't feel it.

MARION THAYER   I've never been in an open boat in my entire life!

EDITH CORSE EVANS   Last week, in Vienna, a fortune teller told me to beware of the water—

CAROLINE NEVILLE   Charles—promise we'll stay together no matter what—

CHARLES CLARKE   I promise, darling—

ELEANOR WIDENER   As long as there's heat and light I'm staying right where we are.

MADELEINE ASTOR   My diamonds! I've forgotten my diamonds!

J. J. ASTOR   Never mind, Maddy—I'll get you much better ones when we get to New York—

135

THE MAJOR   Reminds me of the time I was on the China Sea during the Boxer Rebellion of 1900 when our ship was attacked by a godless horde of Malay pirates—

J. H. ROGERS   Mrs. Cardoza—if anything should happen to me, I'd be very grateful if you could deliver this message to my sister in Ohio

MRS. CARDOZA   I'm sure you'll be all right, Mr. Rogers.

J. H. ROGERS   I count things, ma'am—I count cards and I count lifeboats. There aren't enough. I want my sister to know I was aboard this ship.

MRS. CARDOZA   But your name is on the passenger list, Mr. Rogers—

J. H. ROGERS   My actual name is Jay Yates.

MRS. CARDOZA   The famous card sharper? But I won several hundred dollars from you.

J. H. ROGERS   Our game was interrupted.

   (As they go, Capt. Smith enters, followed by Andrews)

ANDREWS   Captain—

CAPT. SMITH   Yes, Mr. Andrews.

ANDREWS   I'm sure it hasn't escaped your notice, sir, that there are in excess of 22 hundred souls on this ship—

CAPT. SMITH   I'm well aware of that.

ANDREWS   —but space for less than a thousand in the lifeboats.

CAPT. SMITH (stops and turns)   *I* didn't design this ship, Mr. Andrews—

ANDREWS   And *I* didn't instruct the management on the number of boats.

CAPT. SMITH   Evidently 20 boats were enough to satisfy the Line. How many would we need to save every man, woman, and child aboard?

ANDREWS   54. But the Line felt that anything over 20 would have taken away too much deck space from 1st Class. And that means well over half of us are going to die in approximately 90 minutes.

CAPT. SMITH   Not if a ship arrives—

ANDREWS   Do you know of one?

CAPT. SMITH (He continues on)   I'm just on my way to find out.

LIGHTOLLER (Entering)   Captain—all 1st and 2nd Class passengers are proceeding to the Boat Deck as ordered. The 3rd Class have been assembled below on the Well Deck, awaiting instructions.

ANDREWS   Captain, I don't think the passengers and crew fully comprehend their predicament yet. You'll have to tell them, of course—

CAPT. SMITH (He again stops)   Tell them what, Mr. Andrews? That more than twelve hundred of them are already dead? I think not, sir. There would be general panic! They'd kill each other in order to survive!

LIGHTOLLER   Awaiting instructions, Captain—

CAPT. SMITH   What? I want you up top, in charge of loading the boats.

LIGHTOLLER   But the 3rd Class passengers, sir—they're all down below—

CAPT. SMITH   That's not your concern, Mr. Lightoller! Carry on—

LIGHTOLLER   Yes, sir—

   (He goes)

ANDREWS   Are you taking it upon yourself to decide who lives and who dies? I'd remind you that while you are the captain, you were not hired to play God.

CAPT. SMITH   Then let it be God who decides.

ANDREWS   It would appear that God is already leaning toward the 1st Class.

CAPT. SMITH   How so?

ANDREWS   They are closest to the lifeboats, aren't they?

CAPT. SMITH   Then perhaps He'll even the score by sending us a ship.

   (He goes. Ismay enters and glares at Andrews.

   The RADIO ROOM is revealed. "Radio Room; 12:16 am" is displayed. Radioman Bride is hunched over his key, sending a continuous "C.Q.D." as Capt. Smith enters. Andrews will follow shortly)

BRIDE   C-Q-D—Titanic C-Q-D—situation critical—repeat, situation critical—

CAPT. SMITH   Radioman—have you reached any ships—?

BRIDE (Without turning)   Can't you see I'm busy? Go bother the captain—

CAPT. SMITH   This *is* the captain!

   (Bride springs to his feet, forgetting his earphones, which are pulled from his head)

BRIDE   Sorry, sir—

CAPT. SMITH   Sit *down*, Mr.—

BRIDE   Bride, sir. With the Marconi International Marine Radio-telegraphy and—

CAPT. SMITH   Sit *down*, Mr. Bride!

BRIDE   Yes, sir—

CAPT. SMITH   And continue!

BRIDE   Yes, sir—

   (He sits and, reattaching his earphones, resumes sending his "C.Q.D.")

CAPT. SMITH   Have you reached any ships in the immediate vicinity, Mr. Bride?

BRIDE   Six or seven, sir—

    (He consults some scraps of paper)

—the closest seems to be *Carpathia,* a Cunard liner—

CAPT. SMITH   I know *Carpathia,* Mr. Bride—

BRIDE   —They acknowledged our C.Q.D. at 11:58 pm, saying they've turned and are coming hard.

CAPT. SMITH   How far is she?

BRIDE   58 miles, sir.

ANDREWS   That's more than four hours.

CAPT. SMITH   *Carpathia* can't be the only ship in the vicinity, Mr. Bride.

BRIDE   There *was* one other, sir—the *Californian*—her

signal was much stronger than the others—I'd put her within ten miles—but since the accident she hasn't responded.

CAPT. SMITH   Why not?

BRIDE   I don't know, sir.

    (Ismay enters)

ISMAY   E. J.—you've got to do something!

CAPT. SMITH   What do you suggest, Mr. Ismay?

ISMAY   We need another ship here immediately.

CAPT. SMITH   I'm afraid the nearest one is four hours away.

ISMAY   Four hours—! We'll be on the bottom by then!

CAPT. SMITH What about the *Californian,* Mr. Bride—you said that she might be close by—

BRIDE I'm sure she is, sir, but still no response—

ISMAY Why not? You must *demand* a response—!

BRIDE Those smaller ships only carry one radioman, sir—he must have signed off and gone to bed.

ISMAY Well, keep trying, for God's sake!

BRIDE There's a new distress call—S.O.S.—it's hardly ever been used yet. But it's easier to read than the C.Q.D. and I thought—

CAPT. SMITH Try anything you like, Mr. Bride! You must rouse that ship!

BRIDE (Returns to his key) S-O-S—Titanic S-O-S—Situation critical—Come in, *Californian*—Where are you, old man?— Why the hell don't you answer?—

ISMAY
  Surely something can be done to help us . . .

ANDREWS
  Thousands on board
  Trusting and warm

  Roused from their sleep
  Sent up above
  Unsinkable ship
  What is she now?
  What is she now? . . .

ISMAY
  Possibly she won't go down
  Possibly she'll stay afloat
  Possibly all this could come to an end
  On a positive note . . .

ANDREWS
  Not unless the ship could fly
  Not unless we all sprout wings!
  Honestly, sir, I have built her from scratch
  And I know certain things!

ISMAY
  If you know so much
  Why didn't you know to prevent this?
  What's to become of us all
  Now that Providence sent this?
  This is your work, Mr. Andrews
  You have done us in
  Where's her leakproof bulkheads?

Where's *her double skin?*
That's your job!
If someone must take the blame
It is you!
You! . . .

CAPT. SMITH
Innocent folk
Held in our care
Living their lives
Dreaming their dreams
Dreaming their dreams . . .

ISMAY
Possibly a ship will come
Possibly we'll all be saved . . .

ANDREWS
Dammit, sir, listen!
We're hem'rhaging fast!
It's our hull that's been staved!

ISMAY
Couldn't you design it right?
Whoever heard of steel that rips?

ANDREWS
Ismay, I'm just in the bus'ness of building
It's God who sinks ships! . . .

ISMAY
There stands the captain
Who sailed us straight into disaster!

ANDREWS
Oh, now it's the captain's turn
Pray, who urged him to go faster? . . .

  (No answer)

Why then, thank you, Mr. Ismay
For your contribution
Now please pray for some
Miraculous solution!
Your timing is perfect!
Now help us, please
If you can!

CAPT. SMITH
Who called for speed and to break ev'ry record?
Who had to keep all the millionaires happy?

ISMAY
How dare you, Smith?!
I will not stand here indicted!
Who ignored warnings of icebergs when sighted?

  (He turns to Andrews)

Who sir refused to extend up the bulkheads?!

ANDREWS
You, *sir! To give the first class*
Bigger staterooms!

CAPT. SMITH
Who *undermined the position of captain?*

ISMAY
And who took a course too far north for the season?

CAPT. SMITH
And who kept insisting we land ever sooner? . . .

ISMAY
And who should have posted   **ANDREWS**
More lookouts in darkness? . . .   *And who had to have both*

                       The largest and
fastest? . . .
Who did it?!

SMITH
Who did it?!   *Who did it?!*

ISMAY
Who did it?!

ALL THREE
Who did it?!

(Music continues as they reflect; finally:)

ANDREWS
Possibly the Lord will act . . .

CAPT. SMITH
Possibly He will provide . . .

ALL THREE
And indicate how
Our unthinkable fate
Can be somehow denied
Somehow denied . . .

ISMAY (To Andrews)
Your work
No one else's . . .

ANDREWS (To himself; referring to Ismay)
My doing
No one else's . . .

CAPT. SMITH (To himself; quietly)
There's only one captain
And I was in charge . . .
This is my ship
No one else's . . .

(The lights fade)

SCENE 5

AT THE LIFEBOATS

On the BOAT DECK: "Boat Deck; 1:46 am" is displayed. There is a davit indicating a lifeboat position, upstage, right, rear; The ship's railing is also upstage. There is now a very noticeable tilting of the deck.

AT RISE: A line of passengers, all now wearing their

lifebelts, stands waiting to board the lifeboat: 1st-class passengers, including the Astors, Thayers with son, Wideners, Benj. Guggenheim with Mme. Aubert, the Strauses, Mrs. Cardoza, J. H. Rogers, Ismay and the Major. 2nd-class passengers include the Beanes and Charles Clarke and Caroline Neville; 3rd-class passengers include Farrell and the three Kates. They all look around in wonderment and uncertainty, and reacting to the bitter cold. The officers in charge are Lightoller and Murdoch, assisted by Etches and another steward.

LIGHTOLLER Women and children will commence boarding the lifeboat!

MURDOCH Men will please stand back!

(The Thayer family stands immobile; she addresses Jack)

MARION THAYER
You and I are getting in the lifeboat
Father will be staying here a while
It will be like rowing in the Serpentine
Come along now, let us have a smile . . .

(Jack is frozen between the two)

JOHN THAYER
Go along with Mother to the lifeboat . . .

MARION THAYER
John . . .

JOHN THAYER
Don't even say it
I'll be fine . . .
I'll collect you both tomorrow morning

(embracing Jack)
You and this beloved son of mine

MURDOCH & LIGHTOLLER (to Ida Straus)
Madam, step this way into the lifeboat

LIGHTOLLER
Mr. Straus, by all means, take a place . . .

ISIDOR STRAUS
No. I will not go before the younger men.

Ida—you must go now—

IDA STRAUS   What about you?

ISIDOR STRAUS   Ida, please, I'm telling you to get into
the lifeboat!

IDA STRAUS   I refuse.

ISIDOR STRAUS   Refuse? How can you refuse? After 40 years you cannot refuse!

IDA STRAUS   I'm sorry, Isidor, but after 40 years how can I leave you now?

ISIDOR STRAUS   Because you must be saved!

IDA STRAUS   For what? To live without you? Absolutely not!

ISIDOR STRAUS   Ida—

IDA STRAUS   Where you go I go!

MURDOCH, LIGHTOLLER & STEWARD
You must get in   J. J. ASTOR
Please step this way . . .   *Maddie, dear, you must*
                          get in the
                          lifeboat

MURDOCH, LIGHTOLLER & STEWARD
There is no time   ALICE BEANE
Please don't delay   *Edgar, look, we're next to*
                          Mrs. Astor

This is the last to leave
It must be lowered now . . .

    (Add Bellboy)

You must get in   GEORGE WIDENER
Please step this way   *Eleanor you must get in*
the lifeboat

There is no time   CHARLES CLARKE
Please don't delay   *Caroline, come quick,*
                          here is a lifeboat

MURDOCH, LIGHTOLLER, STEWARD, BELLBOY
This is the last to leave   ALL PASSENGERS
It must be lowered now . . .   *Little time remaining, final*
                          lifeboat

    (Kate McGowan & Jim Farrell arrive)

JIM FARRELL   There's got to be a place in that lifeboat. Kate, take it for God's sake!

KATE McGOWAN   I'm not going without you, Jim, I don't want to be a widow before I'm a bride!

JIM FARRELL
You're going to be a lady's maid!
Lady's maid in America!

MURDOCH   This boat needs two men at the oars! You, Mr. Fleet—

FLEET (Boarding the boat)   Yes, sir, thank you, sir!

MURDOCH   You, stoker!

BARRETT   Barrett, sir.

MURDOCH   Mr. Barrett, can you row a boat?

BARRETT   I dunno, sir, I never tried—

JIM FARRELL   I can row, sir! I was a fisherman by trade—

MURDOCH   Then get in, man—hurry!

JIM FARRELL   That I will, sir, thank you, sir—

    (To Barrett, as he boards)

Sorry, mate—

BARRETT   Good luck to you, mate—

EDGAR BEANE   Get into the boat, Alice!

ALICE BEANE   Oh, Edgar—I'm sorry about all those horrible things I—

EDGAR BEANE   Alice, do as I say, dammit!

ALICE BEANE   I love you, Edgar—

ETCHES (To Barrett)   Why'd you give up your seat, lad?— You'll never get a place, now.

BARRETT   He's a passenger, isn't he? They're the ones who've been payin' our wages—

BARRETT	BRIDE	COMPANY
(To the photo of Darlene)		
Be thee well	*It's alive with*	*Hurry now we must*
May the lord who	*A thousand*	*Get in the lifeboat!*
watches all		
Watch over thee we're	*Voices, the*	*Hurry now*
May god's heaven be	*Night is alive*	*Running out of Time!*
Your blanket	*With a thousand*	*(etc.)*
As you softly sleep	*Voices (etc.)*	
Be thee well		
When you're finally in		ANDREWS
My arms you'll		*My work no one else's*
plainly see		
This devoted sailor's heart		
And soul are yours to keep		
Yours to keep!		

OFFICERS
Lower away!!!

COMPANY
Hurry now! There isn't any time!
We'll meet tomorrow
We will find a path
And reach tomorrow, past this day of wrath
We'll be together once again
Cling to your hope and prayers till then . . .

BARRETT (To the photo of his girl)
I'll hold thee closely
As I say good-bye
And keep your image
In my memory's eye
And all this love of ours will soar
Come dawn or danger
We'll meet tomorrow
And have each other evermore

COMPANY
Give us tomorrow
And another hour

Let our reunion
Come within our power . . .

Grant one more chance
To make a start
That we may live for
As we part . . .

BARRETT
Be thee well
May the lord who
watches all
Watch over thee!

BRIDE
The night is alive with a
thousand voices

CHARLES CLARKE
Come say you love me
As I kiss your eyes
Let one brief moment
Make eternal ties . . .

FULL COMPANY
If tomorrow is not in store
Let this embracing
Replace forever
Keep us together
Evermore.

SCENE 8

THE SIDE OF THE SHIP

Similar to Act I, Scene 3, the deck is now tilted. There are thirteen portholes, only four of which are practical and lighted. "2:01 am" is displayed.

AT RISE: J. J. Astor, Benj. Guggenheim, John Thayer and George Widener are looking out at the water.

BENJ. GUGGENHEIM   The boats have all gone, it seems.

JOHN THAYER   I can still see my wife. I told her I'd be following.

BENJ. GUGGENHEIM   Only thing you could do.

J. J. ASTOR   *Mine* actually believed it. Of course, she's only nineteen—

GEORGE WIDENER   Death rarely occurs to the young. Nor does anything else, for that matter.

BENJ. GUGGENHEIM   Rather a pity, actually—it was a terribly good crossing up to now. So many agreeable people.

J. J. ASTOR   A few too many climbers, I thought. Lately I've noticed that anyone with a few million dollars considers himself rich.

BENJ. GUGGENHEIM   Is it possible, do you think, that we have this coming?

JOHN THAYER   The hell you say!

GEORGE WIDENER   For God's sake, Benjamin—what have *we* ever done?

BENJ. GUGGENHEIM   I can't help remembering something Balzac wrote. He said, "Behind every great fortune lies a great crime." So let's confess it. Who wants to start?

(This is met with total silence. Then the lights go out.

Lights up on: Edgar Beane, J. H. Rogers, Fred Barrett and Charles Clarke. "2:06 am" is displayed.)

EDGAR BEANE   That water looks colder than a polar bear's keester and it won't be long before we're in it up to ours. Edgar Beane, hardware.

J. H. ROGERS   Jay Yates, gambler.

EDGAR BEANE   That must be interesting work.

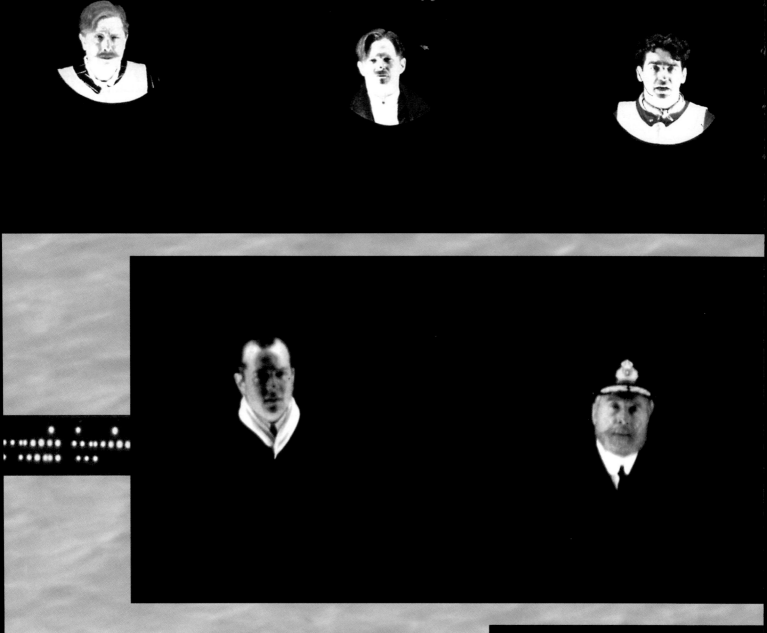

J.H. ROGERS   How about a game of 2-handed stud to pass the time?

EDGAR BEANE   Sure, why not?

J. H. ROGERS   I warn you, I cheat.

EDGAR BEANE   So what? I'm not going to pay you anyway.

BARRETT   That was your wife you were sayin' g'bye to, then?

CHARLES CLARKE   Almost. We were going to be married when we got to New York.

BARRETT   Yeah? I was to be married when I got back to England.

CHARLES CLARKE   It seems we're both going to wind up bachelors.

BARRETT   It could be worse, sir.

CHARLES CLARKE   Really? How?

BARRETT   At least we're not makin' any widows, are we?

CHARLES CLARKE   Good point. What would you gentlemen say to a good stiff drink?

EDGAR BEANE   I'd say one won't be nearly enough.

   (Lights out.

   Lights up on Capt. Smith, Murdoch, Etches and the Bellboy; "2:10 am" is displayed.)

BELLBOY   All 20 boats have been launched, Captain!

CAPT. SMITH   Thank you. You have a remarkably sunny disposition, boy. How old are you?

BELLBOY   14, sir.

CAPT. SMITH   I was a cabin boy at 14. What are you called?

BELLBOY   Edward, sir.

CAPT. SMITH   Really. So am I.

> (The Bellboy goes)

ETCHES   All of the ladies in 1st Class, except one, are safely away, Captain.

CAPT. SMITH   Thank you Mr. Etches.

ETCHES   I'm afraid most of the gentlemen we know are still aboard. There's no hope, I suppose—

> (No response)

I see. Who could have imagined it, sir? Everyone said she was unsinkable.

CAPT. SMITH   Mr. Ismay was fond of boasting that *Titanic* was her own lifeboat.

MURDOCH   That must have been before he used one of the little ones to save his own skin.

CAPT. SMITH   More than anything else the man wanted a legend. Well, now, by God, he's got one.

MURDOCH   Captain—I want you to know that I take full responsibility. I was the ranking officer on the bridge at the time of—if I were a fit master I'd have rammed the iceberg head on. We'd have staved the bow, perhaps lost a few people, but the ship would have survived.

CAPT. SMITH   I'm sure you did what you thought best at the time, Mr. Murdoch.

MURDOCH   You expected more of me, sir—you had every right—but your expectations were misplaced.

> (He goes)

CAPT. SMITH (Lost in his own thoughts)   The truth is I've been uncommonly lucky. In my 43 years at sea I've served on them all, all of the White Star ships—and in all that time I have never been in, nor even seen a shipwreck, nor any other calamity worth speaking of.

> (He goes, leaving Etches alone)

ETCHES (His eyes heavenward)
> *Thousands on board*
> *Each in his class*
> *You are the master of all that must pass*
> *Yours to set course*
> *Yours to command*
> *You hold our souls*
> *In the palm of Your hand*
> *You hold our souls*
> *In the palm of Your . . .*

> (His voice fades out as the light fades quickly to black.)

SCENE 7

THE UPPER PROMENADE DECK.

A railing stretches across the stage. The tilting of the deck has now increased perilously.

AT RISE: "'A' Deck, 2:14 pm" is displayed. Isidor & Ida Straus stand at the rail with Kate Mullins, Kate Murphey, the Millionaires, Edgar Beane, Barrett, and Charles Clark. Hartley plays "Autumn" on the violin. They all exit except for the Strauses.

ISIDOR STRAUS   Are you cold, Momma?

IDA STRAUS   Lately I'm always cold.

ISIDOR STRAUS   Come, I'll blow on your fingers.

IDA STRAUS   Save your breath.

ISIDOR STRAUS   What for?

ETCHES (He approaches with champagne and two glasses)   Mr. Straus—

ISIDOR STRAUS   Mr. Etches—

ETCHES   —Mrs. Straus, a glass of champagne, perhaps?

ISIDOR STRAUS   Champagne? Why? Do you think we have something to celebrate?

ETCHES   I brought the Cristal, 1898. It's the last bottle left.

IDA STRAUS My goodness. It would be a shame to open it.

ETCHES (He opens the bottle and fills the glasses) Under the circumstances, madam, I think it would be a shame not to.

ISIDOR STRAUS Won't you join us for a glass, Mr. Etches?

ETCHES   Later perhaps, sir. I still have my regular people to attend. May I say it's been a great pleasure over the years serving you both?

> (He goes)

ISIDOR STRAUS (He hands her a glass of champagne)   To us.

IDA STRAUS   Who else?

> (As they touch glasses and drink)

IDA STRAUS   You know? You're still a pretty good-looking fella.

ISIDOR STRAUS   I would have to be, to keep such a beautiful wife.
> *Still*
> *The way I love you*
> *Still*
> *Lives in my heart*

IDA STRAUS
> *After all of the years*
> *We've been together*

BOTH
> *Holding our love*
> *Still . . .*

ISIDOR STRAUS
> *The way you move me*
> *Still*
> *Feels as it did*

When you first became mine
Whispered the words

BOTH

"I will" . . .
I loved you then
And I love you
Still

IDA STRAUS

No one else could play your role
Forever know my mind

ISIDOR STRAUS

True companion of my soul
I won't turn from
You I learn from
Still . . .

BOTH

Through fortune's changes
Still
Always we've known . . .

ISIDOR STRAUS

That the promise we made . . .

BOTH

Kept us as one
And will!
I loved you then . . .
And I love you . . .

(He has wrapped his empty champagne glass in his handkerchief and placed it on the deck where he now smashes it under his foot)

Still!

(The scene changes to:)

SCENE 8

THE 1st CLASS SMOKE ROOM & THE DECK ABOVE.

The Smoke Room is revealed below

AT RISE: "1st-class Smoke Room; 2:19 am" is displayed. Thomas Andrews, his jacket and life preserver thrown over a chair, is alone, poring over a set of nautical plans spread over a card table. He appears unaware of his surroundings or even the tilt of the ship. On the mantle is the perfect model of *Titanic*.

Above, on THE TILTING DECK: Capt. Smith has appeared and now calls through a megaphone.

CAPT. SMITH   I declare this vessel lost! From now on it's every man for himself!

(He goes)

ANDREWS

Just a cursory look at the blueprints here
Shows the weaknesses that we have missed
How the water poured in

A three-hundred-foot gash
And caused the bow to flood and to list

And then it filled, to the top
Of our sep'rate watertight compartments
And began to overflow . . .
Because the walls in-between the compartments
Are too low!
She's only sinking because these bulkheads
Stop a deck too low!

But here's a thought! take a line . . .
And extend up the walls to the brink . . .
It's just a small redesign . . .
But once it's done, then I know she can't sink!
Like this! . . . and like this! . . .

    (He is wildly erasing and redrawing lines)

Like this! . . . and then like this! . . .

    (The bellboy enters)

BELLBOY   Mr. Andrews! Aren't you going to make a go of it?

    (As Andrews fails to respond)

Mr. Andrews?!

    (He runs off)

    (The interruption has restored Andrews' reality; he
    retrieves the model ship and stares at it: Cassandra-
    like, he now sees the future.

    Above him, on the BOAT DECK, passengers and crew
    are seen struggling as they attempt the steep climb
    to the stern of the ship)

ANDREWS
The ship will start to plunge beneath the surface
The water lapping at our feet
Down sinks the bow, up flies the stern
To the sky . . .
The panicked people in retreat

A thousand strong, they'll climb up
Toward the aft deck
They'll cling here desp'rately, like bees
To a hive!
Here they'll hold fast
Doomed to the last
Lost and abandoned and all
Still alive . . .

A few of them will hang there
From the railings
As, one by one, they'll drop away!
More than two-hundred-fifty feet
They will fall
And after that, I cannot say
I will not say !

    (The room and the deck above now start a slow
    increase of the tilt, until it is almost too precipitous
    to stand. The furniture begins to slide to the low end
    of the room.)

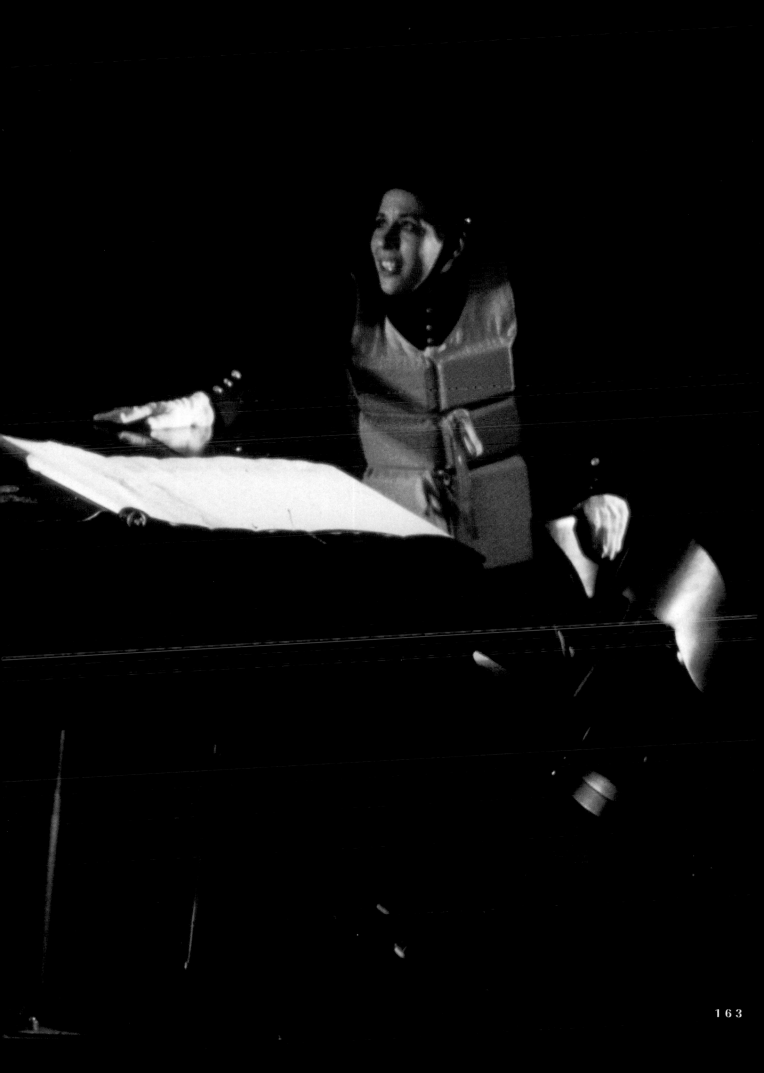

The rest, in swarms, will overrun the boat deck
They'll lose all sense of right and wrong
It will be ev'ry man for himself, all right!
The weak thrown in with all the strong!

First class and third and second
Will mean nothing!
And sheer humanity alone will prevail
One single class
Brute, harsh and crass
That's what will come of the world that set sail . . .

(The veil of madness once again descends)

Autumn . . .
Shall we all meet in the autumn? . . .
Shall we all meet in the autumn? . . .

(The piano now rolls toward him, trapping and crushing him against a bulkhead.

The scene changes:)

SCENE 9

ABOARD THE *CARPATHIA*

One by one, in a line, the survivors—Lightoller, Madeleine Astor, Jim Farrell, Mrs. Cardoza, Alice Beane, Caroline Neville, Kate McGowan, Bride, Ismay, Mme. Aubert, Marion Thayer and her son, Eleanor Widener, Fleet & Henry Etches—all enter. They are wrapped in blankets with the ship's name—*Carpathia*—on them to protect them from their recent exposure in the lifeboats.

"The *Carpathia;* April 15, 1912/8:40 am" is displayed.

LIGHTOLLER   One moment the ship was there—and the next, she was gone.

MADELEINE ASTOR   There were over a thousand poor souls floundering in the freezing water—

JIM FARRELL   We wanted to go back for 'em, of course, to pick 'em up—

MRS. CARDOZA   But they'd've swamped us—then no one could have survived—

ALICE BEANE   The sound they made was deafening—like there was an entire football stadium out there in the dark somewhere.

CAROLINE NEVILLE   And then, after half an hour, it just stopped—

KATE McGOWAN   I'm ashamed to say I was relieved—

BRIDE   I'll hear those voices for the rest of my life—

ISMAY   Why shouldn't I have taken that place in the lifeboat? It would have gone empty.

MARION THAYER   There were more than 450 empty seats in the lifeboats—

MME. AUBERT   It was so very cold—

ELEANOR WIDENER   The women were so brave—alone in the

dark, in the middle of the ocean—

FLEET If only I'd seen that iceberg before it was too late—

ETCHES If only they hadn't kept increasing the speed—

BRIDE If only the *Californian* had heard my call. I stayed with the key 'til the end. They could have saved every man, woman and child aboard!

ISMAY We were only 95 miles from dry land—

CAROLINE NEVILLE When dawn came we could see ice everywhere—it was all bathed in pink. And hundreds of deck chairs floating in the water—

KATE McGOWAN And all o' them poor women and children in 3rd Class who never even made it to the boats—

ETCHES All 50 bellboys, none more than 15 years old, went to their deaths without a whimper.

MRS. CARDOZA All of the musicians who kept on playing "Autumn," right to the very end—

LIGHTOLLER With only 711 survivors, one thousand five hundred and 17 souls had lost their lives.

CAROLINE NEVILLE Including the man I call my husband—

MADELEINE ASTOR And *my* husband—

MARION THAYER And *my* husband—

ELEANOR WIDENER And *my* husband—

ALICE BEANE And *my* husband—

ETCHES In a matter of only a few minutes the largest moving object on earth had totally disappeared.

BRIDE
Fare thee well
May the Lord who watches all watch over thee

May God's heaven be your blanket as you softly sleep . . .

ALL SURVIVORS
Softly sleep . . .

(As they continue, Lightoller, at the end of the line, has obtained the model of Titanic.)
In ev'ry age mankind attempts
To fabricate great works
At once magnificent
And impossible . . .

On desert sands, from mountains of stone
A pyramid!

From flying buttresses alone
A wall of light!
A chapel ceiling
Screaming one man's ecstasy!
One man's ecstasy . . .

Miracles them all!
China's endless wall . . .
Stonehenge, the Parthenon, the Duomo . . .
The aqueducts of Rome

We did not attempt to make
With mammoth blocks of stone
A giant pyramid
No, not a pyramid . . .
Nor gothic walls that radiate with light . . .

Our task was to dream upon
And then create
A floating city! . . .

> (The survivors become silent; only the
> voices of the dead, offstage, are heard.)

THE DEAD (O.S.)
    Floating city! . . .

THE COMPANY
    A human metropolis . . .
    A complete civilization!
    Sleek!
    And fast!
    At once a poem
    And the perfection
    Of physical engineering . . .

    At once a poem
    And the perfection
    Of physical engineering . . .

SCENE 10

SOUTHHAMPTON. THE DOCK

As seen in ACT 1, Scene 1: with the gangway, marked
"WHITE STAR LINE," cutting diagonally across the
stage, leading Off, to the great ship.

AT RISE: The remainder of the Company, all of those
who died, are standing, frozen in time, where they were
first seen.

Now the Survivors walk into their midst, filling in the
gaps where they had once been. When they are in place:

FULL COMPANY
    Farewell, farewell
    Godspeed, Titanic!
    From your berth glide free
    As you plough the deep
    In your arms I'll keep
    Safely west
    May you carry me . . .

    Sail on, sail on
    Great Ship, Titanic!
    Cross the open sea
    Pray the journey's sound
    Till your port be found
    Fortune's winds
    Sing Godspeed to thee . . .
    Fortune's winds
    Sing Godspeed
    To thee!

FINAL CURTAIN

Those Who Perished

Abbing, Anthony
Abbott, Eugene
Abbott, Rossmore
Abelson, Mr. Samson
Adahl, Mauritz
Adams, J.
Ahlin, Johanna
Ahmed, Ali
Aldworth, Mr. C.
Alexander, William
Alhomaki, Ilmari
Ali, William
Allen, William
Allison, Miss L
Allison, Mr. H. J.
Allison, Mrs. H. J.
Allum, Owen G.
Anderson, Albert
Anderson, Alfreda
Anderson, Anders
Anderson, Ebba (child)
Anderson, Ellis
Anderson, Ida Augusta
Anderson, Ingeborg (child)
Anderson, Paul Edvin
Anderson, Samuel
Anderson, Sigrid (child)
Anderson, Sigvard (child)
Anderson, Thor
Andrew, Mr. Edgar
Andrew, Mr. Frank
Andrews, Mr. Thomas
Angheloff, Minko
Anie, Mr. William
Appleton, Mrs. E. D.
Arnold, Joseph
Arnold, Josephine
Aronsson, Ernest Axel A.
Artagaveytia, Mr. Ramon
Ashby, Mr. John
Asim, Adola
Asplund, Carl (child)
Asplund, Charles
Asplund, Gustaf (child)
Asplund, Oscar (child)
Assam, Ali
Astor, Colonel J. J. and
  Manservant
Attala, Malake

Augustsan, Albert
Backstrom, Karl
Badt, Mohamed
Baily, Mr. Percy
Baimbridge, Mr. Chas. R.
Balkic, Cerin
Balls, Mrs. Ada E.
Banfield, Mr. Frederick J.
Banous, Elias
Barbara, Catherine
Barbara, Saude
Barry, Julia
Barton David
Bateman, Mr. Robert J.
Baumann, Mr. J.
Baxter, Mr. Quigg
Beattie, Mr. T.
Beauchamp, Mr. H. J.
Beavan, W. T.
Benson, John Viktor
Berglund, Ivar
Berkeland, Hans
Berriman, Mr. William
Betros, Tannous
Billiard, A. van
Billiard, James (child)
Billiard, Walter (child)
Bjorklund, Ernst
Bjornstrom, Mr. H.
Blackwell, Mr. Stephen Weart
Borebank, Mr. J. J.
Boutandyeff, Guentcho
Botsford, Mr. W. Hull
Boulos, Akar (child)
Boulos, Hanna
Boulos, Sultani
Bourke, Catherine
Bourke, John
Bowen, David
Bowenur, Mr. Solomon
Bracken, Mr. Jas. H.
Brady, Mr. John B.
Braf, Elin Ester
Brandeis, Mr. E.
Braund, Lewis
Braund, Owen
Brewe, Dr Arthur Jackson
Brito, Mr. Jose de
Brobek, Carl R.

Brocklebank, William
Brown, Mr. S.
Brown, Mrs.
Bryhl, Mr. Curt
Buckley, Katherine
Burke, Jeremiah
Burke, Mary
Burns, Mary
Butler, Mr. Reginald
Butt, Major Archibald W.
Byles, Rev.nomas R. D.
Bystrom, Miss Karolina
Cacic, Grego
Cacic, Luka
Cacic, Manda
Cacic, Maria
Calic, Peter
Canavan, Mary
Cann, Erenst
Cannavan, Pat
Car, Jeannie
Caram, Joseph
Caram, Maria
Carbines, Mr. William
Carlson, Carl R.
Carlson, Mr. Frank
Carlsson, August Sigfrid
Carlsson, Julius
Carr, Ellen
Carran, Mr. F. M.
Carran, Mr. J. P.
Carter, Mrs. Lillian
Carter, Rev. Ernest C.
Carver, A.
Case, Mr. Howard B.
Cavendish, Mr. T.W.
Cbronopoulos, Demetrios
Celotti, Francesco
Chaffee, Mr. Herbert F.
Chapman, Mr. Charles
Chapman, Mr. John H.
Chapman, Mrs. Elizabeth
Chartens, David
Chehab, Emir Farres
Chisholm, Mr. Robert
Christmann, Emil
Chronopoulos, Apostolos
Clark, Mr. Walter M.
Clarke, Mr. Charles V.

Clifford, Mr. George Quincy
Coelho, Domingos Fernardeo
Colbert, Patrick
Coleff, Fotio
Coleff, Peyo
Coleridge, Mr. R. C.
Collander, Mr. Erik
Colley, Mr. E. P.
Collyer, Mr. Harvey
Compton, Mr. A. T., Jr.
Conlin, Thos. H.
Connaghton, Michel
Connors, Pat
Conolly, Kate
Cook, Jacob
Cor, Bartol
Cor, Ivan
Cor, Ludovik
Corbett, Mrs. Irene
Corey, Mrs. C. P.
Corn, Harry
Cotterill, Mr. Harry
Coxon, Daniel
Crafton, Mr. John B.
Crease, Ernest James
Cribb, John Hatfield
Crosby, Mr. Edward G.
Cummings, Mr. John Bradley
Dahlberg, Gerda
Dakic, Branko
Danbom, Ernest
Danbom, Gillber (infant)
Danoff, Sigrid
Danoff, Yoto
Dantchoff, Khristo
Davidson, Mr. Thornton
Davies, Alfred
Davies, Evan
Davies, John
Davies, Joseph
Davies, Mr. Charles
Davison, Thomas H.
Deacon, Mr. Percy
Dean, Mr. Bertram F.
del Carlo, Mr. Sebastian
del Carlo, Mrs.
Delalic, Regyo
Denbou, Mr. Herbert
Denkoff, Mito

Dennis, Samuel	Fynney, Mr. Jos.	Hansen, Claus	Jenkin, Mr. Stephen
Dennis, William	Gale, Mr. Harry	Hansen, Henry Damgavd	Jensen, Hans Peter
Dewan, Frank	Gale, Mr. Shadrach	Harbeck, Mr. Wm. H.	Jensen, Nilho R.
Dibden, Mr. William	Gallagher, Martin	Harknett, Alice	Jensen, Svenst L.
Dibo, Elias	Garthfirth, John	Harmer, Abraham	Johann, Markim
Dimic, Jovan	Gaskell, Mr. Alfred	Harper, Mr. John	Johansen, Nils
Dintcheff, Valtcho	Gavey, Mr. Lawrence	Harris, Mr. Henry B.	Johansson, Erik
Dooley, Patrick	Gee, Mr. Arthur	Harris, Mr. Walter	Johansson, Gustaf
Douglas, Mr. W. D.	Gerios, Assaf	Harrison, Mr. W. H.	Johnson, Jakob A.
Downton, Mr. William J.	Gerios, Youssef	Hart, Henry	Johnson, Mr. A.
Doyle, Elin	Gerios, Youssef	Hart, Mr. Benjamin	Johnson, Mr. W.
Drazenovic, Josip	Gheorgheff, Stanio	Heininen, Wendla	Johnsson, Carl
Drew, Mr. James V.	Giglio, Mr. Victor	Hemming, Norah	Johnsson, Malkolm
Dulles, Mr. William C.	Gilbert, Mr. William	Hendekevoic, Ignaz	Johnston, A. G.
Dyker, Adolf	Giles, Mr. Edgar	Henery, Delia	Johnston, Mrs. C. H. (child)
Ecimovic, Joso	Giles, Mr. Fred	Henriksson, Jenny	Johnston, Mrs.
Edwardsson, Gustaf	Giles, Mr. Ralph	Herman, Mr. Samuel	Johnston, William (child)
Eitemiller, Mr. G. F.	Gilinski, Leslie	Hickman, Mr. Leonard	Jones, Mr. C. C
Eklunz, Hans	Gill, Mr. John	Hickman, Mr. Lewis	Jonkoff, Lazor
Ekstrom, Johan	Gillespie, Mr. William	Hickman, Mr. Stanley	Jonsson, Nielo H.
Elias, Joseph	Givard, Mr. Hans K.	Hilliard, Mr. Herbert Henry	Julian, Mr. H. F.
Elsbury, James	Goldschmidt, Mrs. George B.	Hiltunen, Miss Martha	Jusila, Katrina
Emmeth, Thomas	Goldsmith, Frank J.	Hipkins, Mr. W. E.	Jusila, Mari
Enander, Mr. Ingvar	Goldsmith, Nathan	Hocking, Mr. George	Jutel, Henrik Hansen
Evans, Miss E.	Goncalves, Manoel E.	Hocking, Mr. Samuel J.	Kalil, Betros
Everett, Thomas J.	Goodwin, Augusta	Hodges, Mr. Henry P.	Kallio, Nikolai
Fahlstrom Mr. Arne J.	Goodwin, Charles E.	Hoffman, Mr. and two chil-	Kalvig Johannes H.
Farrell, James	Goodwin, Harold (child)	dren (Loto and Louis)	Kantor, Mr. Sehua
Faunthorpe, Mr. Harry	Goodwin, Jessie (child)	Hold, Mr. Stephen	Karajic, Milan
Fillbrook, Mr. Charles	Goodwin, Lillian A.	Holm, John F. A.	Karlson, Nils August
Fischer, Eberhard	Goodwin, Sidney (child)	Holt, Mr. W. F.	Karnes, Mrs. J. F.
Flynn, James	Goodwin, William F. (child)	Holten, Johan	Kassan, M. Housseing
Flynn, John	Graham, Mr.	Holverson, Mr. A. O.	Kassem, Fared
Foley, Joseph	Green, George	Hood, Mr. Ambrose	Keane, Mr. Daniel
Foley, William	Greenberg, Mr. Samuel	Horgan, John	Keefe, Arthur
Ford, Arthur	Gronnestad, Daniel D.	Howard, Mr. Benjamin	Kekic, Tido
Ford, M. W. T. N.	Guest, Robert	Howard, Mrs. Ellen T.	Kelly, James
Ford, Maggie (child)	Guggenheim, Mr Benjamin	Humblin, Adolf	Kelly, James
Ford, Margaret	Gustafson, Alfred	Hunt, Mr. George	Kent, Mr. Edward A.
Ford, Mr. E. W.	Gustafson, Anders	Ilieff, Ylio	Kenyon, Mr. F. R.
Ford, Mrs. D. M.	Gustafson, Johan	Ilmakangas, Ida	Kerane, Andy
Foreman, Mr. B. L.	Gustafsson, Gideon	Imakangas, Pista	Kiernan, John
Fortune, Mr. Charles	Haas, Aloisia	Isham, Mrs. A. E.	Kiernan, Phillip
Fortune, Mr. Mark	Hagardon, Kate	Ivanoff, Konio	Kilgannon, Thomas
Fortune, Mrs. Mark	Hagarty, Nora	Jacobsohn Mr. Sidney S.	Kink, Maria
Fox, Mr. Stanley H.	Hagland, Ingvald O.	Jakob, Mr. Birnbaum	Kink, Vincenz
Fox, Patrick	Hagland, Konrad R.	Jardin, Jose Netto	Kirkland, Rev. Charles L
Franklin, Charles	Hakkurainen, Pekko	Jarvis, Mr. John D.	Klaber, Mr. Herman
Franklin, Mr. T. P.	Hale, Mr. Reginald	Jean Nassr, Saade	Klasen, Gertrud (child)
Funk, Miss Annie	Hampe, Leon	Jefferys, Mr. Clifford	Klasen, Hilda
Futrelle, Mr. J.	Hanna, Mansour	Jefferys, Mr. Ernest	Klasen, Klas A. Mona, Mae A.

Kraeff, Thodor
Killner, Mr. John Henrik
Laitinen, Mr. William
Laitinen, Sofia
Laleff, Kristo
Lam, Len
Lamb, Mr. J. J.
Lambert-Williams, Mr. Fletcher Fellows
Lane, Patrick
Laroche, Mr. Joseph
Larson, Viktor
Larsson, Bengt Edvin
Larsson, Edvard
Lefebre, Frances
Lefebre, Henry (child)
Lefebre, Ida (child)
Lefebre, Ida (child)
Lefebre, Mathilde (child)
Leinonen, Antti
Lemberopoulos, Peter
Lemom, Denis
Lemon, Mary
Leonard, Mr. L
Lester, J.
Levy, Mr. R. J.
Lewy, Mr. E. G.
Lemon, Mr. Robert W. N.
Lindablom, August
Lindahl, Agda
Lindell, Edvard B.
Lindell, Elin
Lihan, Michel
Ling, Lee
Lingan, Mr. John
Lingrey Mr Edward
Lithman, Simon
Lobb, Cordelia
Lobb, William A.
Lockyer, Edward
Long, Mr. Milton C.
Loring, Mr. J. H.
Louch, Mr. Charles
Lovell, John
Lundahl, John
Mack, Mrs. Mary
MacKay, George W.
Maenpaa, Matti
Maguire, Mr. J. E.
Mahon, Delia
Maisner, Simon
Makinen, Kalle
Malachard, Mr. Noel

Malinoff, Nicola
Mallet, Mr. A.
Mangan, Mary
Mangiavacchi, Mr. Emilio
Mantvila, Mr. Joseph
Marinko, Dmitri
Markoff, Marin
Marshall, Mr.
Marvin, Mr. D. W.
Matthews, Mr. W. J.
Maybery, Mr. Frank H.
McCaffry, Mr. T.
McCarthy, Mr. Timothy J.
McCrae, Mr. Arthur G.
McCrie, Mr. James
McElroy, Michel
McGowan, Katherine
McKane, Mr. Peter D.
McMahon, Martin
McNamee, Eileen
McNamee, Neal
Meanwell, Marian O.
Mechan, John
Meek, Annie L.
Melkebuk, Philemon
Meo, Alfonso
Meyer, Mr. August
Meyer, Mr. Edgar J.
Miles, Frank
Millet, Mr. Frank D.
Milling, Mr. Jacob C.
Minkoff, Lazar
Mirko, Dika
Missahan, Dr. W. E.
Misseff, Ivan
Mitchell, Mr. Henry
Mitkoff, Mito
Moch, Mr. Phillip E.
Moen, Sigurd H.
Molson, Mr. H. Markland
Monbarek, Hanna
Moore, Leonard C.
Moore, Mr. Clarence and Manservant
Moran, James
Morawick, Dr. Ernest
Morgan, Daniel J.
Morley, William
Morrow, Thomas
Moussa, Mantoura
Moutal, Rahamin
Mudd, Mr. Thomas C.
Murdlin, Joseph

Myhrman, Oliver
Myles, Mr. Thomas F.
Naidenoff, Penko
Nancarrow, W. H.
Nankoff, Minko
Nasr, Mustafa
Nasser, Mr. Nicolas
Natsch, Mr. Charles
Naughton, Hannah
Nedeco, Petroff
Nemagh, Robert
Nenkoff, Christo
Nesson, Mr. Israel
Newell, Mr. A. W.
Nicholls, Mr. Joseph C.
Nicholson, Mr. A. S.
Nieminen, Manta
Niklasen, Sander
Nilsson, August F.
Nirva, Isak
Norman, Mr. Robert D.
Nosworthy, Richard C.
O'Brien, Denis
O'Brien, Thomas
O'Connell, Pat D.
O'Connor, Maurice
O'Connor, Pat
O'Donaghue, Bert
O'Neill, Bridget
O'Sullivan, Bridget
O'Leary, Norah
Olsen, Carl
Olsen, Henry
Olsen, Ole M.
Olson, Elon
Olsson, Elida
Olsson, John
Oreskovic, Jeko
Oreskovic, Luka
Oreskovic, Maria
Orsen, Sirayanian
Ortin, Zakarian
Ostby, Mr. E. C
Otter, Mr. Richard
Ovies, Mr. S.
Pacruic, Mate
Pacruic, Tome
Pain, Dr. Alfred
Panula, Eino
Panula, Ernesti
Panula, Juho
Panula, Maria
Panula, Sanni

Panula, Urhu (child)
Panula, William (infant)
Parker, Mr. Clifford R.
Parr, Mr. M. H. W.
Partner, Mr. Austin
Pasic, Jakob
Paulsson, Alma C
Paulsson, Gosta (child)
Paulsson, Paul (child)
Paulsson, Stina (child)
Paulsson, Torborg (child)
Pavlovic, Stefo
Payne, Mr. V.
Peacock, Alfred
Peacock, Treasteall (child)
Peacode, Treasteall
Pearce, Ernest
Pears, Mr. Thomas
Peduzzi, Joseph
Pelsmaker, Alfons de
Peltomaki, Nikolai
Penasco, Mr. Victor
Pengelly, Mr. Frederick
Pentcho, Petroff
Perkin, John Henry
Pernot, Mr. Rene
Person, Ernest
Peruschitz, Rev. Jos. M.
Peter, Anna
Peter, Mike
Peters, Katie
Peterson, Ellen
Peterson, Johan
Peterson, Marius
Petranec, Matilda
Petterson, Olaf
Phillips, Mr. Robert
Plotcharsky, Vasil
Ponesell, Mr. Martin
Porter, Mr. Walter Chamberlain
Potchett, George
Pulbaun, Mr. Frank
Radeff, Alexander
Rafoul, Baccos
Raibid, Razi
Reed, James George
Reeves, Mr. David
Renouf, Mr. Peter H.
Reuchlin, Mr. Jonkheer, J. G.
Reynolds, Harold
Rice, Albert (child)
Rice, Arthur (child)

Rice, Eric (child)
Rice, Eugene (child)
Rice, George (child)
Rice, Margaret
Richard, Mr. Emile
Rintamaki, Matti
Risien, Emma
Risien, Samuel
Robins, Alexander
Robins, Charity
Roebling, Mr. Washington A., 2nd
Rogers, Mr. Harry
Rogers, William John
Rood, Mr. Hugh R.
Rosblom, Helene
Rosblom, Salfi (child)
Rosblom, Viktor
Ross, Mr. J. Hugo
Rothschild, Mr. M.
Rouse, Richard H.
Rowe, Mr. Alfred
Rummstvedt, Kristian
Rush, Alfred George J.
Ryan, Patrick
Ryerson, Mr. Arthur
Saad, Amin
Sadlier, Matt
Sadowitz, Harry
Sage, Ada (child)
Sage, Annie
Sage, Constance (child)
Sage, Dorothy
Sage, Douglas
Sage, Frederick
Sage, George
Sage, John
Sage, Stella
Sage, Thomas (child)
Sage, William (child)
Salander, Carl
Salonen, Werner
Samaan, Elias
Samaan, Hanna
Samaan, Youssef
Sarkis, Lahowd
Sarkis, Mardirosian
Sather, Sinon
Saundercock, W. H.
Sawyer, Frederick
Scanlan, James
Scrota, Maurice

Sdycoff, Todor
Sedgwick, Mr. C. F. W.
Seman Betros (child)
Shabini, Georges
Sharp, Mr. Percival
Shaughnesay, Pat
Shedid, Daher
Shellard, Frederick
Shorney, Charles
Sihvola, Antti
Silvey, Mr. William B.
Simmons, John
Sivic, Husen
Sjostedt, Mr. Ernest A.
Skoog, Anna
Skoog, Carl (child)
Skoog, Harald (child)
Skoog, Mabel (child)
Skoog, Margret (child)
Skoog, William
Slabenoff, Petco
Sleiman, Attalla
Slemen, Mr. Richard J.
Slocovski, Selman
Smart, Mr. John M.
Smiljanic, Mile
Smith, Mr. Augustus
Smith, Mr. J. Clinch
Smith, Mr. L P.
Smith, Mr. R. W.
Sobey, Mr. Hayden
Sohole, Peter
Solvang, Lena Jacobsen
Somerton, Francis W.
Sop, Jules
Spector, Woolf
Spencer, Mr. W. A.
Spinner, Henry
Staneff, Ivan
Stankovic, Jovan
Stanley, E. R. Mr.
Stanton, Mr. S. Ward
Stead, Mr. W. T.
Stewart, Mr. A. A.
Stokes, Mr. Phillip J.
Stone, Mrs. George M. and Maid
Storey, T. Mr.
Stoyehoff, Ilia
Stoytcho, Mihoff
Strandberg, Ida
Straus, Mr. Isidor and

Manservant
Straus, Mrs. Isidor and Maid
Strilic, Ivan
Strom, Selma (child)
Sutehall, Henry
Sutton, Mr. Frederick
Svensen, Olaf
Svensson, Johan
Swane, Mr. George
Sweet, Mr. George
Syntakoff, Stanko
Tannous, Daler
Tannous, Thomas
Taussig, Mr. Emil
Taussig, Mrs. Emil
Thayer, Mr. J. B.
Theobald, Thomas
Thomas, Alex
Thomas, CharlesP
Thomas, John
Thorne, Mr. G.
Thorneycroft, Percival
Tikkanen, Juho
Tobin, Roger
Todoroff, Lalio
Tomlin, Ernest P.
Tonfik, Nahli
Torber, Ernest
Torfa, Assad
Tronpiansky, Mr. Moses A.
Tupin, M. Dorothy
Turcin, Stefan
Turpin, Mr. William J.
Uruchurtu, Mr. M. R.
Useher,Baulner
Uzelas, Jovo
Van de Velde, Joseph
Van de Walle, Nestor
Van der Hoef, Mr. Wyckoff
Van der Planke, Augusta Vander
Van der Planke, Emilie Vander
Van der Planke, Jules Vander
Van der Planke, Leon Vander
Van der Steen, Leo
Van Impe, Catharine (child)
Van Impe, Jacob
Van Impe, Rosalie
Vassilios, Catavelas
Veale, Mr. James
Vereruysse, Victor

Vestrom, Huld A. A.
Vook, Janko
Waelens, Achille
Walker, Mr. W. Anderson
Ware, Frederick
Ware, Mr. John James
Ware, Mr. William J.
Warren, Charles W.
Warren, Mr. F. M.
Wazli, Yousif
Webber, James
Weir, Mr. J.
Weisz, Mr. Leopold
Weller, Abi
Wende, Olof Edvin
Wenzel, Zinhart
West, Miss Barbara
West, Miss Constance
West, Mr. E. Arthur
Wheadon, Mr. Edward
Wheeler, Mr. Edwin
White, Mr. Percival W.
White, Mr. Richard F.
Wick, Mr. George D.
Wick, Mrs. George D.
Widegrin, Charles
Widener, Mr. Harry
Widener, Mrs. George D. and Maid
Wiklund, Jacob A.
Wiklund, Karl F.
Willey, Edward
Williams, Harry
Williams, Leslie
Williams, Mr. Duane
Windelov, Einar
Wirz, Albert
Wiseman, Philip
Wittenrongel, Camille
Wright, Mr. George
Yazbeck, Antoni
Youssef Georges (child)
Youssef, Brahim
Youssef, Hanne
Zabour, Hileni
Zabour, Tamini
Zakarian, Maprieder
Zievens, Renee
Zimmermann, Leo

SHELTER DECK C
SALOON DECK D
UPPER DECK E
MIDDLE DECK F
LOWER DECK G

WHITE STAR LINE
STATE ROOM
D
STATE ROOM
No. Berth

SECOND CLASS PROMENADE
ENGINEERS PROMENADE
FIRST

RAISED ROOF

TURBINA
FAN ENGINE
CASING
FANS
TANK ROOM
RECIPROC
E CASING
BOILER
CASING

DOME OVER
RC ENTR
ELEC
WINCH
TANK ROOM
OFFICER
MESS

OVER 1ST C SMOKE RM

FIRST CLASS

ELEC CRANE

VERANDAH AND PALM COURT
FIRST CLASS
1ST CLASS
CLOAK ROOM

FANS
TURB
ENG
CAS
ENGINE CASING
BOILER CASING

VERANDAH AND PALM COURT
SMOKE ROOM
ENTRANCE
LOUNGE PANTRY Y BAR

ELEC CRANE

FIRST CLASS